Archaeology,
Heritage, and
Civic Engagement

Archaeology, Heritage, and Civic Engagement

Working toward the Public Good

Barbara J. Little
Paul A. Shackel

Left Coast
Press Inc.
Walnut Creek,
California

green press
INITIATIVE

Left Coast Press, Inc. is committed to preserving ancient forests and natural resources. We elected to print this title on 30% post consumer recycled paper, processed chlorine free. As a result, for this printing, we have saved:

2 Trees (40' tall and 6-8" diameter)
1 Million BTUs of Total Energy
173 Pounds of Greenhouse Gases
938 Gallons of Wastewater
63 Pounds of Solid Waste

Left Coast Press, Inc. made this paper choice because our printer, Thomson-Shore, Inc., is a member of Green Press Initiative, a nonprofit program dedicated to supporting authors, publishers, and suppliers in their efforts to reduce their use of fiber obtained from endangered forests.

For more information, visit www.greenpressinitiative.org

Environmental impact estimates were made using the Environmental Defense Paper Calculator. For more information visit: www.papercalculator.org.

Left Coast Press Inc.

LEFT COAST PRESS, INC.
1630 North Main Street, #400
Walnut Creek, CA 94596
http://www.LCoastPress.com

ISBN 978-1-59874-637-2   hardcover
ISBN 978-1-59874-638-9   paperback
ISBN 978-1-59874-639-6   institutional eBook
ISBN 978-1-61132-771-7   consumer eBook

Library of Congress Cataloging-in-Publication Data
Little, Barbara J.
  Archaeology, heritage, and civic engagement : working toward the public good / Barbara J. Little, Paul A. Shackel.
      pages cm
  Summary: "The definition of "public archaeology" has expanded in recent years to include archaeologists' collaborations with and within communities and activities in support of education, civic renewal, peacebuilding, and social justice. Barbara Little and Paul Shackel, long-term leaders in the growth of a civically-engaged, relevant archaeology, outline a future trajectory for the field in this concise, thoughtful volume. Drawing from the archaeological study of race and labor, among other examples, the authors explore this crucial opportunity and responsibility, then point the way for the discipline to contribute to the contemporary public good"-- Provided by publisher.
  Includes bibliographical references and index.
    ISBN 978-1-59874-637-2 (hardback) — ISBN 978-1-59874-638-9 (paperback) — ISBN 978-1-59874-639-6 (institutional ebook) — ISBN 978-1-61132-771-7 (consumer ebook)
  1. Community archaeology. 2. Archaeology—Social aspects. 3. Cultural property—Social aspects. 4. Common good. I. Shackel, Paul A. II. Title.
  CC77.C66L57 2014
  930.1--dc23
                              2013042900

Printed in the United States of America

∞ ™ The paper used in this publication meets the minimum requirements of American National Standard for Information Sciences—Permanence of Paper for Printed Library Materials, ANSI/NISO Z39.48–1992.

Copyediting: Susan Schmid
Design and Production: Detta Penna

Contents

List of Figures and Tables

Acknowledgments

We have thought about writing this book for some time. Although we were both trained in the scientific method of the New Archaeology, we have been part of a discipline that has changed and expanded over the past few decades. While archaeology can be performed for the sake of knowledge alone, it can have more complicated applications, especially when we involve living communities. We can begin to think about the uses of the past and we can be active agents who use heritage to make the world a better place—for the public good. There are many who came before us and were brave enough to challenge the paradigms of the discipline. They made a difference by making heritage relevant to communities and addressing social justice issues. We appreciate this groundbreaking work and recognize that we stand on the shoulders of our predecessors.

Along the path to making this book a reality were many people who helped to shape how we think about heritage and archaeology. Many of these scholars are cited throughout the book. A special thank you goes to our colleagues and students for discussing some of these issues and inspiring us. Thanks also go to Mike Roller and to Adam Fracchia for their able assistance in preparing the final manuscript. We are pleased to have Kristin Sullivan's photo on the cover, and extend our thanks to Susan Walters Schmid for her copyediting skills and to Detta Penna for the book's design. We would also like to thank Mitch Allen for his patience as we completed this book.

Introduction

Freedom.

It is difficult to invoke a concept more embedded in the imagined heritage of the United States. This one word, with its many meanings and many genealogies, is emblematic of the complexity of heritage and its uses. It is our entry point into a discussion about intersections among heritage, justice, peacebuilding, civic engagement, and the "working through" that people need to do to come to public judgment within a democracy.

We begin with a brief heritage story and an aspiration.

Monticello, near Charlottesville, Virginia, is the iconic home of Thomas Jefferson, writer of the Declaration of Independence, one of the "Founding Fathers" of the United States, and a wealthy slaveholder. In his essay "Labor and Leisure at Monticello," anthropologist Eric Gable (2009) writes about identity, race, privilege, and the inadvertent power of heritage in his analysis of some visitor programs at the site.

At Monticello, the staff has worked diligently in recent years to ensure that there are relevant representations of the past available to African American visitors; it is not Gable's intent (or ours) to call into question staff members' sincere desire to make their site a more inclusive place. Instead, Gable presents an observation about the insidious nature of assumptions about race. At the time of his research, Monticello was selling the first in a series of postcards commemorating captive and enslaved residents. That first postcard showed a portrait of the enslaved blacksmith Isaac Jefferson, and his portrait was also featured on a brochure about the enslaved workers of Mulberry Row, the plantation's industrial hub. Monticello is not alone in presenting its black history for black audiences, making the implicit assumption that white people already have their ancestral history in the person of Mr. Jefferson. In this way, whites identify with privilege and blacks identify with disenfranchisement. Adding black history into a site from which it was previously excluded appears to be a progressive step toward inclusion. Yet, this well-intentioned effort seems akin to what feminist scholars deride as the "add women and stir" approach to history to make the point that the underlying structures of representation matter and must themselves be explored and rehabilitated.

Gable (2009) observes that southern plantations, as places where aristocratic privilege was based on absolute disenfranchisement, continue to be sites of national celebration that produce national identity in the United States. He argues that the reason for the longevity and influence of such plantations is that they are inadvertent white identity shrines, where segregated racial identity is reinforced. He asks how we can use such places to think about the nature of privilege, suggesting that we shift the location of identify from race to class by creating a way for white visitors to identify with the labor of blacks.

How can such re-thinking and revised categories and representations encourage changes in our conversations about freedom? About struggle? About the lessons of the past for the present?

Archaeologist Terrance Weik (2012) suggests in *The Archaeology of Anti-slavery Resistance* that the study of resistance to slavery gives us the opportunity to learn what freedom can mean. The long-term struggle for freedom from slavery compels a richer and more complex view of freedom. A more liberating view of freedom would be grounded in a plurality of cultures, beyond that of modern capitalism intent on individualism. Weik (2012, 153). summarizes the kind of aspiration that is coming to define the purpose of public archaeology:

> archaeologists are helping to challenge monolithic notions such as the idea that the "American experience" was the story of founding fathers in search of freedom. The experience also involved the denial of freedoms and the struggles of Africans, native societies, the working class, and poor people (of different cultures) to regain their dignity and rights in colonial and modern societies. *The discourse can help people move toward a postcolonial present by encouraging them to challenge opportunists who marshal notions of freedom and resistance as convenient rallying cries that feed global domination and ideologies of privilege* (emphasis added).

The heritage arena is one location for such a discourse. Archaeologists and other heritage practitioners and culture workers contribute some of the voices. There is an increasingly recognized need for other voices to translate among the myriad languages spoken by academics, expert practitioners, citizens engaged and participating in civil society, and policymakers. Those groups of individuals cannot be mutually exclusive if the discourse is to be intelligible and productive.

We consider ourselves members of a very large community of heritage workers. Within this community, there are those who would identify easily with that label: archaeologists, museum curators, historians, applied anthropologists, and many more. There are also others who frame their work differently but whose work intersects with heritage through culturally informed conflict resolution; democracy-building; social, economic and environmental justice; and other fields where the intersections between past and present heritage matter. We appreciate the diverse experience and expertise of our colleagues, and we want to tap into the energy and commitment their work can bring to the heritage arena through analysis of and ideas about interrelated topics such as identity, rhetoric and narrative, civic engagement, democracy, reconciliation, collaboration, conflict resolution, and peacebuilding.

We have organized this book loosely along the lines of a civic engagement strategy for deliberative democracy, described by Marshall Ganz (2011) in his essay "Public Narrative, Collective Action, and Power." This explanation of action-oriented public narrative as storytelling echoes one of the methods community organizers use to identify issues of common concern and to lead people to action.

First, we each share our own story—the *story of self*—to explain why we care about an issue. Then we pool our concerns with those of a broad range of colleagues to create the *story of us*, to identify the story we all can share. Finally, we tell the *story of now*. We translate our shared ideas and ambitions into actions, not in the future, but now. This layered storytelling is iterative and cumulative, and the resulting dialogue leads to co-imagined possibilities, a common goal from shared experiences, and action. We listen to colleagues in an imperfect sampling—some case studies and some thought pieces—pulling together threads we see as compatible with heritage as healing, transformative, creative, and outside of the traditional boundaries of disciplines and practices.

PART ONE

Story of Self

Here we give a little personal background about our own work, we place ourselves in a tradition of anthropology that has shifted to take responsibility both for the consequences of its own past and for action in the world today, and finally, we offer some definitions that are relevant throughout the book.

Archaeology, Heritage, and Civic Engagement, Barbara J. Little and Paul A. Shackel, p. 15–16.

Chapter 1

Story of Self

Story of Self: Some Reflections from the Authors

We were trained as archaeologists to practice archaeology as a defined discipline with boundaries. The accompanying restrictions made less and less sense to us as we explored the potential of historical archaeology, which we believed required that those boundaries be crossed. We can each recall many times in our early careers when we were told that what we were doing might be interesting but it was not archaeology. This often insistent critique came from every direction. A "stay inside your box" message enforces the orderliness of academic divisions and departments and works against effective or sustained cross-disciplinary collaboration. On the practical side, however, two things must be acknowledged: it is difficult to get a job if one does not fit inside the boxes for which practitioners are being hired, and it is impossible to be well-versed and up-to-date in any reasonably broad field of knowledge. Yet, we persist.

Paul

Archaeology means different things to different people, but most people hope to make a connection to the past as a way to find meaning in their lives today. I was trained in the tradition of the New Archaeology—a mid-twentieth-century, science movement in the discipline away from description and historical context and toward explanation and generalizations about human behavior.

I became aware of the political power of the past and the role of archaeology while discovering critical theory in the 1980s as I worked on the Archaeology in Annapolis project. In the 1990s, while employed at Harpers Ferry National Historical Park as an archaeologist, I participated in research that focused on examining the roots of industrial capitalism and the inequalities and discontent in a wage labor system. The important contribution of this research was to connect the past to the present and show that many of the inequalities in today's society began with the Industrial Revolution. While we can boast of many modern conveniences, such as mass manufactured goods, they came at the price of alienation of labor in the factory system. Experiencing the way the National Park Service selectively interpreted this important episode of U.S. history, it became more apparent to me how the past is presented through a certain lens and that present-day actors influence the meaning of the past.

In the early 1990s, many professionals continued to argue adamantly that the goal of archaeology was to find a true and objective past. While there are still many today who hold to that position, the world of archaeology in the United States changed dramatically in the 1990s. Many different communities were obtaining a greater say in how their pasts were treated and interpreted. The Native American Graves Protection and Repatriation Act (NAGPRA) and the incidents behind the creation of the African Burial Ground National Monument in New York City opened the door to a new type of public archaeology—civic engagement. Communities could control their past and their destinies. It became increasingly clear to me that archaeologists and their work could make a difference in the present by addressing and acting on many of the "isms" that exist today in our society, including racism, sexism, and ageism.

In the early 2000s I was invited by the New Philadelphia Association in western Illinois to rediscover the heritage of an African American community known as New Philadelphia. This large-scale project was a collaboration with the University of Illinois and the Illinois State Museum (see chapter 6), and it provided the opportunity to use portions of the civic engagement "toolkit" to make the community more aware of the deep roots of racism that existed in the region. I thought that our work might also lead to anti-racism activities in the community. However, most people were skeptical and did not initially participate in the project, and many challenged our findings. It was the Internet that became the key instrument in the democratization of knowledge. We used the project's website to describe a clear path to how we collected our historical and archaeological data, and to demonstrate how the town had developed within a racist climate. As we describe in chapter 7, climbing the civic engagement pyramid was not easy, nor was it a natural ascent for community members. However, because of the democratization of the project findings, the New Philadelphia Association is taking responsibility for becoming a more inclusive organization, while promoting a more inclusive past. Archaeology served as a touchstone that connected the past with the present and enabled the community to act to change its social and political climate. It remains a work in progress.

In the 2010s, I turned once again to my interest in connecting past and present labor inequalities. Class, ethnicity, and racism all play a major role in the way people are identified and treated in the labor force. A team that includes several graduate students is working in the coal patch towns of northeastern Pennsylvania, collecting oral histories and performing archaeology. Examining the historical records reveals that in the late nineteenth century, embedded racism influenced the treatment of new immigrants from eastern and southern Europe who came to labor in the coal mines. Today, this region is receiving a new influx of Latino immigrants to work in minimum wage jobs because most youth of European descent have left for better opportunities in New York City, Philadelphia, and Baltimore. These new immigrants are generally receiving the same hostile treatment the European immigrants received several generations earlier. The challenge for the project is to make the established community aware of the injustices of the past and its connection to the treatment of new immigrants today. Perhaps this work in the community will alleviate some of the racism still evident. It is also a work in progress.

Barbara

Archaeology is an extraordinarily diversified practice. I find it useful (albeit impractical) to be curious about a broad range of its theoretical stances, methods, and practical applications. I am fascinated that archaeology belongs to both the sciences and the humanities and that, in spite of the synthesizing power available to our discipline, the fragments of the practice fight and claw against each other. I want the insights that archaeology reveals about the ways in which material and ideological realities complicate each other. Archaeological heritage is similar to every other category of tangible heritage in reflecting that complication.

My initial training in archaeology, like Paul's, was very much embedded in the New Archaeology. I was drawn to the field partly because I was looking for explanations about how we got to be where we are as a society. Eventually such questions led me to become far more interested in historical archaeology than in the exoticized and far-removed past being offered to me as an undergraduate. However, the lens of the New Archaeology's brand of "science" and the objective distance it appeared to require were initially appealing because they seemed powerful. Power was important in the 1970s, particularly for a young woman mystified and irritated that there were few welcoming places for a woman in the academic world. I followed that science path briefly, delving into mathematical modeling and such because I was interested in complex problems. I was, and still am, excited about the possibilities of anthropological archaeology. I see no boundaries to anthropology, and thus no boundaries to its archaeological branch. I am an anthropologist first, an intellectual identity that prompts me to keep looking for intersections and connections.

I remain interested in complex problems and cultivate a high tolerance for ambiguity. Feminist theory introduced me to the deep questioning of shared narratives that I carry with me. That interest was not rooted in academic training but in curiosity stimulated by my daily experience. It is lived experience that has inspired the direction of my work. My central research questions are: "What heritage matters and why?" and "How do we use it?" As a member of the Archaeology in Annapolis project lead by Mark Leone, I learned about critical theory and the aspiration to use archaeology as a tool to free people from the ways in which historical narrative can entrap us in the present. I have remained interested in public outreach and involvement and in the broader relevance of heritage. Through my work as an employee of the National Park Service (NPS), I became interested in official designations and public memory. While I do not speak for the NPS in this book or in many of my other publications, one important exception is the book *Public Benefits of Archaeology* (Little 2002), which was an outgrowth of a conference sponsored by the NPS and partners in 1995. It was difficult to find a publisher for that book because the conventional wisdom in the field was that archaeologists were not particularly interested in the public and the book would be of no interest in the discipline. Instead, as we have witnessed, public archaeology has expanded and thrived in remarkable ways. Continuing in the vein of public benefits, I have been interested in the relevance and usefulness of archaeology (Little 2007, 2010, 2012) and have wondered how archaeologists, in collaboration with others, can contribute to the work of peace and justice (Little 2009, 2011, 2013).

How we, as a society, acknowledge and use the tangible parts of our heritage becomes a powerful force in social, cultural, and political life. Heritage constitutes a complex public sphere that provides opportunities to employ heritage work for the common good, and that is why we offer so many possible connections in this book.

Paul and I have been exploring our joint interest in social justice and continue to strive to move up the civic engagement ladder ourselves so we can use our strengths and our privilege to contribute to peace and justice. We have been inspired by antiracism work and the aspirations of restorative justice across the globe. We are on a journey to become more active citizens in addition to more effectively using our skills as commentators and observers.

A handful of years ago, our goal for *Archaeology as a Tool of Civic Engagement* (Little and Shackel 2007) was to encourage archaeologists to think about effective ways to participate in the civic renewal movement, including community building, the creation of social capital, and active citizen engagement in community and civic life. The contributors to that volume were committed to making stories about heritage fully inclusive and to creating a useable and interconnected heritage that is civically engaging in that it calls a citizenry to appreciate the worthiness of all people's histories and to become aware of historical roots and present-day manifestations of contemporary social justice issues. One connecting thread is raising consciousness about the past and connecting it to the present, particularly with the intention of using archaeological histories as pathways toward restorative justice. A socially useful heritage can stimulate and empower both local community members and visitors to make historically informed judgments about heritage and the ways that we use it in the present. This is an important and growing commitment in archaeology. This book is our next step.

Intersections

In our introduction, we offered a quote from anthropologist Terrance Weik in which he refers to the postcolonial present and our social aspiration to emerge from global colonial relationships. The academic literature currently favors the antecedent "post," which seems to us an optimistic label, and a potentially misleading one. For example, when politicians speak of postconflict, we presume that they do not really mean that once the shooting stops the problems disappear. A post period can last a surprisingly long time. In his work on conflict resolution and peace building, Kevin Avruch (2012) draws on Harold Isaac's characterization of the post-World War II disintegration of power systems. Isaacs (1975) identified these as postcolonial, postimperial, postrevolutionary (referring to the fragility of the USSR and China), and postillusionary (referring to the illusion of white supremacy).

We are especially interested in the last, because we believe that it remains foundational to many social and economic inequalities. If the structural foundations of inequality are interconnected and the rhetorical devices used to sustain them are similar, then truly disrupting and dismantling the illusions of white supremacy will also disrupt and destabilize the illusory justification for interlocking oppressions. We are not under the illusion that there is some sort of ideal natural order that will reappear in some way, but we do believe that we have the power to intentionally change our stories and our democracy.

Isaacs (1975, 19) wrote of the postillusionary society:

> In the United States, the breakdown of the worldwide white supremacy system after 1945 brought down like pricked balloons a whole cluster of illusions about the nature of the American society and raised in new ways and on a new scale the question of the character of the "American" identity. It opened up a time of wrenching change in all group relations within the society and within every group the beginning of an equally wrenching re-examination of itself.

Heritage holds, and upholds, illusions and aspirations; it also encompasses imagined and invented traditions and intentionality. We advocate for intentionally working toward peace; economic, social, and cultural justice; and environmental justice. We appreciate that such justice is a moving target, and that points on the horizon toward which we want to move may become blurred and indistinct. And yet, there is still a horizon that we might truly call a postillusionary society.

Shifts in Our Profession

As much as anthropological archaeology has changed over the past several decades, it continues to change, broadening its scope as both a science and a humanity, expanding its knowledge-focused questions and its social and cultural meanings. Archaeological scholarship and practice continue to explore the roles of practitioners as participants and collaborators in work that is far larger than archaeology done for the sake of archaeological science alone. The meanings of our terms have changed. "Public archaeology," for example, today means something far broader than archaeology that is completed to comply with legal and regulatory requirements or paid for by public funds. It is broader than archaeologists going public to share research results. Public archaeology also includes archaeologists' collaborations with and within communities, and activities in support of education, civic renewal, peace, and justice. This change has come about as archaeologists as heritage practitioners have become increasingly aware of their social and political context. Our grand ambitions speak to a vision of integrating our practice with our common problems. Barbara Little and Larry Zimmerman (2010) have proposed that this trend reflects a quest for wisdom. At least some archaeologists have been helped to see the value of such a quest through work with Native peoples and the cultural values maintained by many indigenous societies.

An increasing number of our colleagues call for creating a civically engaged archaeology that serves the public interest, however difficult that interest is to define. Various subfields of archaeology seek to change mainstream practice. Feminist, Indigenous, antiracist, vindicationist, and Marxist archaeologists offer powerful models that share some goals and methods for rehabilitating archaeology from its colonial and androcentric roots. Sonya Atalay (2006, 284) describes a shared goal this way:

> If our goal is to decolonize archaeology, we must then continue to explore ways to create an ethical and socially just practice of archaeological research—one that is in synch with and contributes to the goals, aims, hopes, and curiosities of the communities whose past and heritage are under study, using methods and practices that are harmonious with their own worldviews, traditional knowledges, and lifeways.

In her book *Black Feminist Archaeology*, Whitney Battle-Baptiste (2011, 31) asks how archaeology can overcome the distrust frequently felt by descendant communities and become trustworthy. Her ambition is to "begin to tell a story that is not just about archaeology or artifacts, but about people and places, women and men, leisure and labor, with details that can be relevant to contemporary struggles for social justice and liberation."

Anthropology has a mixed history of supporting and confronting injustice. Although rooted in colonialism, anthropologists have spent considerable energy undoing the racial typologies created by their predecessors. Anthropology is rooted in, but not wholly defined by, the western natural history tra-

dition that encouraged social observers to classify and compare human populations. By the 1830s, Samuel Morton became the authority on explaining
racial differences with his book *Crania Americana* published in 1839 (Thomas
2000, 38–42). Later, E. B. Tyler and Lewis Henry Morgan became proponents
of social Darwinian theory that aided in creating and reinforcing human racial typologies. Europeans naturalized their new racial attitudes by focusing
on physical differences and concluded that Africans and Indians were a lesser
form of human beings dictated by the laws of nature or God-given attributes
(Smedley 1998, 694).

While many anthropologists backed such racial typologies, some scholars
worked to dismantle these views. In 1897, Franz Boas questioned the premise
behind unilinear evolution, and he challenged the notion that race was bio-
logically fixed and permanent and that people could be ranked in proximity
to apes (Mukhopadhyay and Moses 1997, 518). Many historians of anthropology see Boas's *The Mind of the Primitive Man* (1911) as an influential publication that introduced cultural relativism and muticulturalism as important
concepts in anthropological thinking. Boas (1911) stressed the importance
of environment over heredity in creating variation in human populations.
His work challenged the celebration of western civilization and stressed the
importance of other cultures and experiences as valid cultural expressions
(Roseberry 1992, 848; Visweswaran 1998, 70). In *Changes in Bodily Form of
Descendants of Immigrants* (1912), Boas demonstrated that morphological
features, including core racial indicators like head form, could change in a
single generation because of nutritional, environmental, or cultural factors
(Blakey 1987; Mukhopadhyay and Moses 1997, 518). Paul Rabinow (1992, 60)
observed that "Boas' arguments against racial hierarchies and racial thinking
have thoroughly carried the theoretical day."

After World War II, American anthropologists continued to argue against
the old classifications of racial construction and supported a socially and culturally constructed form of race. In 1952, UNESCO rejected the linkage between
sociocultural capacities and biology (Mukhopadhyay and Moses 1997, 519).
While racism has hardly disappeared from the American landscape, race is no
longer a scientifically credible position in anthropology (Rabinow 1992, 60).

The American Anthropological Association (AAA) has continued this
thread of antiracism scholarship with a multiyear, multimedia project entitled
"Race. Are We So Different?," which consists of a traveling exhibit, publications, a resource-rich website, dialogue techniques, and associated outreach

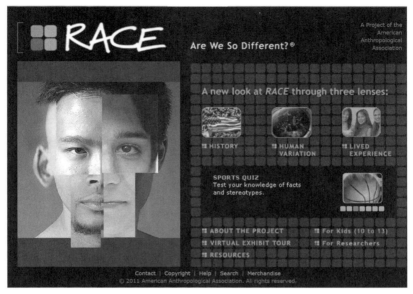

Figure 1.1   American Anthropological Association's Race Project web site. (http://www.understandingrace.org/home.html).

(see figure 1.1). In 2010, the AAA sponsored the symposium "New National Dialogue on Race" held at the Cannon House Office Building in Washington, DC, to engage policymakers. The symposium was cosponsored by the Congressional Black Caucus, Hispanic Conference, Asian Pacific American Caucus, and Humanities Caucus. Yolanda Moses, former president of the AAA and chair of the race project, explained that the project was bringing together the best science and the best cultural work to address the problem: "We created race and racism so how can we change it?"

These efforts are aimed at raising the national level of conversation to equip people to hold meaningful dialogues about race and racism. At the 2012 AAA annual meeting, Jacquelyn A. Lewis-Harris and Moses provided an update on the project. In the communities where museums have hosted the traveling exhibit, the exhibit's intention is being realized as docents lead talking circles about race. Afterwards participants are asking the museums about what will happen next, indicating that they are increasingly ready to talk about race and racism. Teachers and museum educators, as well as the project team, have learned how to talk with people from disparate backgrounds who hold a wide variety of opinions, a skill necessary for facilitating difficult conversations.

While some anthropologists continue to address issues of race, others focus on matters related to social justice, such as poverty, work, violence, homelessness, and repatriation (Checker 2002, 94–105; Chollett 1999, 19–47; Nas 1994, 35–40; Rosenberger 1999, 447–481). Such work becomes a call for social justice when scholars begin to advocate on behalf of the people they study, or when others take up their advocacy and commit themselves to social change. Dialogue around difficult topics is increasingly valuable at heritage sites, and heritage workers will need to develop their skills for facilitating such conversations. We will discuss this sort of dialogue in several places in this book.

Peace and Violence: Some Definitions

We will refer to peace and to different forms of violence throughout this book, so it is important that we provide some definitions.

More than a generation ago, Kenneth Boulding (1978, 13) defined *stable peace* as "a situation in which the probability of war is so small that it does not really enter into the calculations of any of the people involved." Stable peace is not simply the absence of conflict or the presence of deterrence, but it is a state of being where we expect to resolve our differences through dialogue and diplomacy. In a stable peace, violent resolutions are actually unthinkable. Although Boulding focused mainly on nations, his definition included other kinds of social groups so that we can use his concept of stable peace to apply within a nation to think about whether peace between groups and between individuals is stable.

In its glossary, the United States Institute of Peace (Snodderly 2011, 40) provides the following entry for *peace*:

> The word "peace" evokes complex, sometimes contradictory, interpretations and reactions. For some, peace means the absence of conflict. For others it means the end of violence or the formal cessation of hostilities; for still others, the return to resolving conflict by political means. Some define peace as the attainment of justice and social stability; for others it is economic well-being and basic freedom. Peacemaking can be a dynamic process of ending conflict through negotiation or mediation. Peace is often unstable, as sources of conflict are seldom completely resolved or eliminated. Since conflict is inherent in the human condition, the striving for peace is particularly strong in times of violent conflict.

That said, a willingness to accommodate perpetrators of violence without resolving the sources of conflict—sometimes called "peace at any price"—may lead to greater conflict later.

Unstable peace is a kind of truce that is enforced by mutual fear of violence. Stable peace precludes violence, including the threat of violence. In two different articles Johan Galtung provides analytical definitions for *structural violence* (1969) and *cultural violence* (1990), contrasting each with *direct violence* (physical and psychological) yet showing how much they are connected to it. Structural violence is embedded in social structures of oppression, such as racism, sexism, homophobia, and elitism that do harm by preventing people from meeting their basic needs. Cultural violence is any aspect of culture that is used to legitimize direct or structural violence. We want to emphasize that a desirable stable peace precludes both structural and cultural violence.

In his *Outline of a Theory of Practice*, Pierre Bourdieu (1977) defined symbolic violence within his social model as a disguised legitimization of violence. Although symbolic violence may be a more recognizable concept in social science and contemporary political discourse, we prefer to use Galtung's model and language. He uses the image of a "violence triangle" to show that direct violence, structural violence, and cultural violence are causally connected and support each other. The triangle is important conceptually because any of its points can represent a source of provocation or escalation of other types of violence.

In its definition of *peacebuilding*, the United States Institute of Peace glossary includes the idea that (Snodderly 2011, 40): "[P]eacebuilding involves a transformation toward more manageable, peaceful relationships and governance structures—the long-term process of addressing root causes and effects, reconciling differences, normalizing relations, and building institutions that can manage conflict without resorting to violence." Building peace and addressing issues of restorative justice requires that the sources of violence be dismantled. Because heritage can and does support both violence and peace, heritage practitioners need to decide what sort of work they intend to practice. We will never escape the fact that there are unintended consequences of our choices and actions, but we can consider the possibilities more fully at the outset of a project and strive for outcomes that reject violence and support peace.

PART TWO

Story of Us

Creating a shared story requires that we listen to the stories of others, pool our common concerns, and identify the story we share to create the story of us.

The "us" we are listening to includes colleagues in archaeology and heritage and in other fields such as rhetoric, communication, current affairs, environmental advocacy, civic engagement, service learning, and peacebuilding. These stories come from the world of higher education, from museums, from government, from for-profit and non-profit companies, and from practice and theory. The common concern is working towards the public good.

The following chapters range quite broadly and yet there is much we have left out. We hope that readers will call on their own experiences, expertise, and interests to keep expanding and sharing the story of us.

Archaeology, Heritage, and Civic Engagement, Barbara J. Little and Paul A. Shackel, p. 29–30.

Chapter 2

What Does it Mean to Live in the Anthropocene?

Merging Culture and Nature in a New Epoch

Earth scientists are poised to recognize that within the last two hundred years we have come into a new geological epoch—the Anthropocene—to acknowledge the degree to which humans have transformed the earth's surface and caused environmental change. The Anthropocene follows the Holocene, which followed the Pleistocene, each of which are epochs in the Quaternary period of time starting 2.6 million years ago (Zalasiewicz et al. 2011). The substantial growth of cities is one of the defining characteristics of the new epoch. The massive effects of human action include erosion and sedimentation as the result of activities such as deforestation as well as increasing ocean acidity due to dissolution of increased carbon dioxide into the atmosphere. In their essay "The Anthropocene: a new epoch of geological time?," Zalasiewicz and others (2011) note, "The Anthropocene is here treated as a geological phenomenon, comparable to some of the great events of the Earth's deep past. But, the driving force for the component global changes is firmly centered in human behaviour, particularly in social, political, and economic spheres."

What does it mean to live in the Anthropocene? We believe it calls for all of us with an interest in our surroundings—whether natural or built—to work together. There is a paradigm shift underway in the environmental movement. Some contemporary environmentalists are challenging the traditional (albeit overstated) Green attitude that human beings are the scourge of planet Earth and are adopting a more balanced attitude. We will call these folks the "modern greens." In *Rambunctious Garden: Saving Nature in a Post-Wild World*, Emma Marris (2011) challenges the notion that there is anything pristine about what we call wilderness. The modern greens have taken seriously findings that indigenous people have always influenced and managed the environment and that consequently there is nothing akin to the "Garden of Eden" to which we might strive to "restore" ecological conditions. These modern greens currently are having discussions that remind us of passionate arguments among preservationists about the correct period of significance for a building, whether to strip away additions to reveal original fabric, and whether or how to represent layers of a building's history.

Modern greens recognize that nature lives not only in protected areas but in urban areas and indeed all around us, that humans are integral to the natural world, and that separating the natural from the artificial makes no sense in terms of either management or everyday life. This explicit recognition that humans are essential to ecosystems is a radical shift away from the framework and the "nature-first" narrative that has long dominated the politics of the Green movement. Modern greens such as Minteer and Pyne (2012) are pragmatists, recognizing that people value nature in different ways and for different purposes. There is increasing acknowledgment that people have always used, enjoyed, and exploited nature.

Marris (2011) proposes gardening as the appropriate metaphor for a reoriented environmental movement. She wants to introduce joy into our relationship with the earth and distance the movement from the catastrophic hospice mentality that has bemoaned the earth dying at the hands of humans. She emphasizes that humility is the only reasonable approach, as it is clear that humans are shortsighted and always inept.

Ben Minteer and Stephen Pyne (2012, 9) call for a new narrative for American environmentalism. They argue that the traditional narrative and ethical framework are becoming irrelevant to conservation practice: "The informing narrative is not simply one between the wild and the wasted, but between old and new economies, and between human health and nature." In recognizing that humans have entered a new global epoch of their own making within the last 200 years, they want to reclaim a pragmatic approach. As they see it, changing things in a healthy direction for the environment requires reviving a fuller participation of citizenry and collective decision making. In order to respond to developments across the world, local people must take actions that respond to local conditions. The United Nations Development Programme (2012) has recognized the power and necessity of local action in its Equator Prize for community-based initiatives. Winning projects reduce poverty through conservation and sustainable use of biodiversity. Ten years of award-worthy projects demonstrate that such projects are not only possible but are actually being accomplished.

When historic preservationists write about heritage, we are often thinking implicitly about cultural heritage. Nature as heritage is in the background, and it may be seen as a separate political issue requiring separate political action. On the one hand, we may identify ourselves as preservationists who work as cultural heritage managers, working to preserve the tangible remnants and reminders of historically significant places. On the other hand, we may think of ourselves as environmentalists, concerned about issues such as climate change, ocean acidification, species extinction, and so forth. Or we may think of preservationists and environmentalists as competing, as if our metaphorical parallel universes were in fact separate.

Judging by work in the field for the last several decades, it is not uncommon for cultural heritage professionals to feel as if cultural preservation takes a backseat to environmentalism. The feeling of being less visible, less valued by the larger public, and less potent politically can get in the way of integrating complementary movements. Our common aspirations for positive peace and environmental justice remain divided when we cannot integrate our efforts and join forces.

Peace through Shared Environmental Responsibility

In her edited volume *Life and Death Matters: Human Rights, Environment, and Social Justice*, Barbara Johnston (2011) provides powerful, detailed examples of some severe biocultural problems, including agricultural conflicts, war, long-term effects of radiation, climate change, and the dire circumstances surrounding water and water rights. One of the lessons in that volume is that, while chaos might be a necessary ingredient in crisis, it is not necessarily the endpoint for human environmental emergencies. Johnston (2011, 15) asks what she calls the crucial question of our time: "Can we build environmentally sound and socially just solutions to our problems in ways that minimize or prevent the incidence of violent conflict?" How indeed do we attain the positive peace of justice and social stability without violence and how do we sustain it? We are raising the parallel question of how interests in heritage can be transformed into the dismantling of structural and cultural violence rooted in past inequalities but supported by present day relationships and material conditions. We believe our question and Johnston's are intertwined. There are innumerable answers to these questions, most of which remain to be constructed; but, there are attempts being made in communities across the globe.

The field of environmental peacemaking is based on the idea that the common need for a healthy environment can support peacebuilding in conflict zones. Some archaeologists have worked to create common ground based on cultural heritage, helping to bridge even violently polarized communities. Israeli and Palestinian archaeologists, as well as others, have been working towards archaeology as common ground. In their article "Heritage and Reconciliation," Sandra Scham and Adel Yahya (2003) describe a project based on reflexivity and dialogue between archaeologists in warring nations. Funded by the U.S. Department of State through the 1998 Wye River Accords, their project was intended to examine the common heritage of Israelis and Palestinians. Building on dialogues like those Scham and Yahya describe are agreements supporting the peace process, including an agreement on the disposition of archaeological collections following the future establishment of a Palestinian state. This remarkable achievement lays out the principles of repatriation of artifacts and control of archaeological sites in a region where the past is an extremely volatile topic (Bohannon 2008; Sullivan and North-Hager 2008). Such intentional efforts to explore how archaeology might be used to bridge divides are important as archaeology and other tangible manifestations of heritage become politicized all over the globe.

Focusing attention on concerns of mutual interest can help jurisdictions both desire and achieve peaceful cooperation. One strategy of environmental peacemaking is the implementation of Transboundary Protected Areas (TBPA). These areas transcend political boundaries and are dedicated to the protection and management of biological diversity, indigenous cultures, and cultural resources with the goal of promoting peace and cooperation. The strategy behind TBPAs is to transform disputed border areas and develop them into conservation zones with joint responsibility for governance. The removal of border fences and walls allows for the free movement of people, the migration of animals, and the protection of commonly valued cultures and cultural resources. This strategy can work if all parties see joint conservation as beneficial. TBPAs can also promote sustainable development and generate goodwill between neighboring countries (Ali 2010; National Geographic 2011).

TBPAs are also known as "peace parks," a term first used in 1932 when Waterton Lakes National Park in Canada (established 1895) and Glacier National Park in the United States (established 1910) combined their efforts to create Waterton-Glacier International Peace Park (see figure 2.1 [2.0]). It was a mostly symbolic gesture celebrating the long peace between the two countries (Tanner et al. 2007, 183). More recently, peace parks have developed as a mechanism to achieve conflict resolution. Over the past several decades the International Union for Conservation of Nature (IUCN) has been a major supporter of these parks' establishment. In 1988, the IUCN's World Commission on Protected Areas identified at least seventy protected areas in sixty-five countries. In 2007, the United Nations Environment Programme's World Conservation Monitoring Centre identified 227 TPBAs (Peace Park Foundation 2011). Nelson Mandela (2011) proclaimed, "In a world beset by conflicts and division, peace is one of the cornerstones of the future. Peace parks are a building block in this process, not only in our region, but potentially in the entire world."

The focus of peace parks has been the development of environmental conservation zones. With the increased development of these sanctuaries, there is a growing realization that a balance needs to be struck between environment, culture, and people. Some anthropologists have criticized the lobbying efforts of three large international conservation organizations—Nature Conservancy, World Wildlife Fund, and Conservation International—indicating that they are neglecting the indigenous people whose land they are protecting (Ali 2007, 15). Peace Parks provide a different way to think about borders, but recognize that borderlands for peace are still contested spaces. Practitioners in postconflict zones are starting to understand that:

> cultural heritage policies in post-conflict zones cannot proceed in isolation but must be incorporated within the broader objectives of redevelopment and recovery, including accommodation of cultural diversity and human rights....A holistic approach, as suggested above, to the restoration of the built environment and the socio-cultural and economic needs of the population can only be achieved when wider goals of cultural sovereignty, multiculturalism and security are also addressed. (Logan et al 2010, 17)

Figure 2.1   A 25-foot swath cut into the forest marks the international boundary between the United States and Canada at the Waterton-Glacier International Peace Park. By international agreement, this swath is maintained wherever the border is forested. (Photograph by David Restivo, NPS. Licensing terms: http://creativecommons.org/licenses/by/2.0/deed.en.)

An Archaeological Peace Park in the Making

El Pilar is a large ancient Mayan city on the Belize River that was inhabited from 800 BCE until at least 1000 CE. Twenty thousand people lived there, tending gardens surrounded by both forest and agricultural fields (figure 2.2). The 120-acre site straddles a disputed border between Guatemala and Belize. It was placed on the World Monuments Fund's watch list in 1996 due to excessive threats to the site. Both countries developed management plans by 2006, and currently, the site is encompassed by the 5000-acre El Pilar Archaeological Reserve for Maya Flora and Fauna, which celebrates the heritage of the forest and sustainable forest gardens. Work at El Pilar emphasizes collaboration among scholars and local stakeholders as well as international cooperation across the border (figure 2.3). Anabel Ford, director of the MesoAmerican Research Center at the University of California, Santa Barbara, and president of Exploring Solutions Past: The Maya Forest Alliance, is a leading proponent of a binational El Pilar Peace Park. The aspirations for El Pilar contrast with the standard, "Maya tourism narrative…emphasizing great temples and great art"

Figure 2.2   The entrance from Belize to the El Pilar Archaeological Reserve for Maya Flora and Fauna. (Image Courtesy of Michael Glassow, El Pilar Project.)

(Ford 2011, 263) in that it raises the knowledge and practices of local people as important examples and lessons about sustainable farming. It also offers lessons about cultural persistence, and confronts a popular dominant narrative that the Mayan civilization collapsed and failed. The peace park, as such, is a work in progress, but the binational park is in place.

Many locations can serve purposes similar to those of peace parks by promoting learning about alternative ways of being in the world, ways that promote peacebuilding instead of violence and dialogue instead of conflict-laden posturing.

Chapter 3

Heritage, Civic Engagement, and Social Justice

What Is Heritage?

Heritage is a difficult thing to define. Despite attempts by specialists to draw boundaries around what is and is not heritage, the keepers of any particular heritage—the people who use it, shape it, remember it, and forget it—are likely to have their own definitions.

In *Heritage: Management, Interpretation, Identity*, Peter Howard (2003, 1) offers this definition: "Heritage is taken to include everything that people want to save, from clean air to morris dancing, including material culture and nature. It is all-pervasive, and concerns everyone. Much of it divides people." This perfectly reasonable definition immediately raises more questions because there are things some people want to forget or destroy while others want to save and celebrate those very same things. While much heritage divides people, it is also true that much heritage unites people, so it can simultaneously act as social glue and repellant.

We propose a friendly amendment to Howard's definition, to understand heritage (loosely) as whatever matters to people today that provides some connection between past and present. Heritage, of course, is both deep and shallow in terms of time, and it includes the tangible and intangible in culture and nature. Heritage is fluid in the "moving target" sense, what matters can seem to some to come out of nowhere when it appears to dredge up a forgotten or neglected past.

Archaeology, Heritage, and Civic Engagement, Barbara J. Little and Paul A. Shackel, p. 39–52.

39

Because we are archaeologists, our conversation often defaults to archaeological examples, and we are convinced that our field is remarkable for its breadth and depth and for its capacity to bridge the sciences and the humanities. We conceive of the archaeological and built heritage broadly. We understand it to mean not only that which is already uncovered or cared for in a conventional archaeological sense, but also that which remains to be discovered, because that material—extensive, unidentified, unrecognized, undocumented—does matter. In what has become the standard approach to heritage management in the United States, it matters until someone with the power to decide makes the decision that it does not matter. If it does not matter, then the physical traces of the heritage are not deemed worthy of study, preservation, or memory and can be destroyed. This power to destroy as well as to preserve is embedded in our preservation laws and practice, but it does not originate in such laws. The law is embedded in cultural practice concerning how we confront, embrace, absorb, and reject our past, and the paths that past is called upon to support.

Heritage that Hurts/Heritage that Heals

Dissonance. Discord. Contestation. Cultural heritage workers have observed repeatedly the contestations and discord that pervade heritage issues. We recognize heritage as dangerous and difficult terrain. Heritage disciplines have studied and participated in contested meanings of the past and its representations in the present, from repatriation struggles over human remains and objects to identity struggles over naming and preserving. Our diagnoses are often focused on the conflict and on the exclusionary and divisive qualities of heritage. Heritage conflicts are not abstract, but are intensely meaningful to the communities and individuals involved in them, heightening the importance of ethical engagement.

It is commonly accepted now that heritage and identity are deeply intertwined. Marta Anico and Elsa Peralta in their book *Heritage and Identity* (2009) summarize this view: "[W]ho we are very much results from what we have selected from the past and chosen to retain in the present." They continue, connecting heritage, identity, power, and materiality:

> Identities, in order to be effective, have to have some kind of materiality; the totems that symbolize the solidarity felt by generations of heteroge-

neous individuals towards a unifying narrative of belonging. In this context, heritage provides a rather effective material and symbolic support for these narratives, both serving as a resource for the representation of identities and a place for its performance....Heritage, in this sense, is closely linked with power and is an influential device in the construction of nation-states as well as in the identity politics led by multiple groups that are globally situated (1).

While we support most of this statement, we suggest that materiality in the sense of physically tangibility is not actually necessary for effective identity. The UNESCO Convention for the Safeguarding of the Intangible Cultural Heritage recognizes the widespread importance of skilled crafts, performed arts, and other intangible expressions of culture. Certainly the materiality of sites, buildings, objects, and structures is often deeply meaningful. In "Monuments and Memory, Made and Unmade," Robert Nelson and Margaret Olin (2003) explore connections between monuments and social memory, emphasizing their function in connecting past and present to make claims for the future. They argue that: "Because a monument can achieve a powerful symbolic agency, to damage it, much less to obliterate it, constitutes a personal and communal violation with serious consequences." While the destruction of mere things is commonplace in our takeout and throwaway world, attacking a monument threatens a society's sense of itself and its past (2–3)."

The same level of threat is perceived with an attack on the abstractions and imaginaries with which we commemorate our versions of the past—our histories, our beliefs, our knowings—all of which constitute the meanings we create for the heritage we recognize. Threats to choices about which histories matter, how we go about creating and discovering them, and the ways in which they are presented and shared are as serious as threats to tangible fabric.

Ways of knowing can become serious points of contention, as systems of expertise come into contact where power relations are unequal. A generation ago, K. Anne Pyburn and Richard Wilk (1995) saw the importance of professionals to engage with local communities during any archaeological project. They explained that archaeologists need to gauge negative impacts their work might have on communities and that they have an ethical responsibility to mitigate those impacts. Such principled concern with the power dynamics of outsider experts has been ongoing, if uneven, throughout the heritage professions. More recently, in "Cultural Diversity, Cultural Heritage and Human

Rights" William Logan (2012) has argued that heritage management ought to evolve as a human rights-based practice. In pointing out that heritage professionals need to think about the broader social, economic, and political context of their work, he affirms a widespread consensus in the disciplines that has been gaining strength for decades. Professionals working at significant places need to understand how their work can potentially impact local communities, indigenous peoples, and ethnic communities.

Because of power imbalances, official heritage intervention can undermine community cohesion and identity. Those in control of the dominant narrative may insist on reinforcing their views of history, which can reinforce long-standing prejudices and inequalities. At the same time, subordinated groups may counter those claims and advocate versions of the past that include their own sense of heritage. The scale of heritage to be articulated at any particular site may also be a concern for communities. Whether to emphasize a local community's unique characteristics or highlight aspects that reflect universal values is an important decision for many groups. The issues are complex and the situations are always in flux. While the outcomes of engaging communities in these heritage issues may be quite productive, that is neither automatic nor guaranteed.

The development of heritage and the promotion of heritage sites are essentially political acts. Heritage connotes authenticity although the way it is developed and negotiated is often about a group's relationship to power. Places of heritage can be centers that heighten dialogue, or create significant rifts between groups that may have very different memories of a place or events. Decisions are made to promote one form of heritage over another, and academics, politicians, or influential community leaders often influence and support these decisions. In many instances, minority voices are muted, and sometimes one form of heritage is privileged over a community's living cultures.

In his essay "Co-produced Histories: Mapping the Uses and Narratives of History in the Tourist Age," Nikolas Glover (2008, 117) writes that the struggle over the control of a place's meaning often comes down to the issue of authority versus authenticity. In this distinction, the concept of authority is connected to a form of education, critical thinking, and the globalized uses of heritage. Authenticity is linked to the local dimension of historic or cultural sites. Glover explains that locals can claim knowledge associated with both authority and authenticity. But in internal struggles, the polarization is often clearer. In many postcolonial societies, a large majority of academic experts will belong to the ruling ethnic group—for example, the white Creole population in South America. The claim to professional authority will, in such cases, be aligned along ethnic or class lines, as the indigenous groups lay counterclaims in terms of authenticity (117).

Scholarship and claims to authority are always open to contestation. While subjugated people may not be in command of the authority or the claim to authenticity, they can decide what they accept and how to use the narratives of the past. At the same time, authenticity is never inherent in a place or culture, but is created by context. Authenticity is ascribed value, and once an object, place, or culture is assumed to be authentic it becomes associated with a sense of the past (Glover 2008, 117).

The distinction here between authority and authenticity corresponds to a contrast between top-down and bottom-up heritage. While some sort of contrast makes sense to us, we are not at all convinced that the heritage fields have yet come up with appropriate language because the connotations of the words authentic and authority are laden with value judgments that are potentially misleading and prejudicial. Authenticity implies a deep truth—always risky when referring to heritage. When heritage is paired with identities of struggle engaged in at the bottom of a power hierarchy, it risks incorporating the foggy judgment of nostalgia for the rightness of "the people" and its accompanying sentimentality. We do acknowledge that authentic heritage in the "hidden history" sense is often that which has been suppressed or blurred by power relations. The erasure is often incomplete, providing the possibility of reclaiming and reasserting those hidden histories as important heritage.

Authentic heritage often is painful history and "heritage that hurts" has become one of the recognizable categories of heritage studies, especially as it pertains to the tourism industry or to educational curricula. The promise and potential of transformation form the basis of our recognition that the painful past is worth confronting and learning from. In an immediate and deeply personal way, this is the argument for the truth and reconciliation efforts in nations recovering from debilitating violence. Sharon MacDonald (2009) is one of many voices recognizing and advocating the move to incorporate more unsettling memories into public contexts. In her essay "Unsettling Memories: Intervention and Controversy over Difficult Public Heritage," she contrasts two cases ripe with colliding visions about the past: one concerns efforts to turn a major Nazi-era government building in Nuremberg into a shopping and leisure center (figure 3.1), and the other concerns museum display of

Figure 3.1   Congress Hall today during the Volksfest, or People's Fair. (Image courtesy of Sharon MacDonald.)

items from the transatlantic slave trade in Tampa, Florida. MacDonald (103) suggests that unsettlement —by which she means the incorporation of more unsettling memories into public contexts—makes heritage available as an ethical space, "capable not only of affirming certain identities but of prompting more complex, often humanistic and cosmopolitan, reflection on matters such as the relationship between past, present and future, and on the nature of heritage itself."

But not all heritage is about identity, nor is it all divisive or disturbing. Commonly recognized categories of heritage values, such as those acknowledged by the *Australia ICOMOS Burra Charter, 2013*, include aesthetic, scientific, historic, spiritual, and social—the last of which would include identity. In 1995, the Getty Conservation Institute began an intensive study on the values and economics of cultural heritage (de la Torre 2002). They recognized that the democratization of heritage has increased its complexity and that the professional field needs to share power and collaborate with those who are not experts in conservation. The Getty project started with the assumption that "heritage conservation is an integral part of civil society" and one can characterize opposing views of heritage as a "contingent-universal debate" (Avrami et al. 2000, 3). The contingent side views cultural heritage as a social construction strongly influenced by relations of power and identity specific to a time and place. Those who favor the universal view embrace the long-standing idea that heritage has universal qualities.

We believe that both views are valid and, given the malleable meanings of heritage, apply simultaneously. As Uffe Juul Jensen (2000, 43) writes:

> Cultural heritage has two faces. It can be—and often is—constructed
> to support the activities or dominance of powerful groups or nations at
> the expense of other groups or nations. But cultural heritage can also
> be constructed with deference to an ideal of human flourishing that has
> been recognized by various, often opposite, traditions and communi-
> ties throughout Western history….Cultural heritage constructed from
> different positions and standpoints in a multi-cultural world thus may
> contribute to the fulfillment of universal human aspirations.

We are of the opinion that winning the "contingent-universal" debate is irrelevant, and we instead advocate for intentional reframing of the heritage project as a peacebuilding enterprise. Lourdes Arizpe (2000, 32) identifies a key question for a *new global cultural commons*: "How do we enhance the value of cultural heritage to safeguard it and to use it to build cultural understanding instead of cultural trenches?"

Virtual Heritage/Authentic Challenge

Professional discourse around heritage concerns both tangible and intangible heritage. The longest standing heritage professions have developed through expertise in real-world material manifestations: archaeological sites, formal and vernacular landscapes, buildings, structures, and artifacts. More recently, heritage professions in a growing number of countries explicitly recognize and include intangible cultural expressions, such as crafts and performance arts. But what about virtual heritage? Does technology present us with simply one more tool to edit and present what we choose to highlight and preserve, or might it lead us into a new kind of heritage?

New media have changed the ways in which people interact with each other and how they define their own communities. What is the relationship of traditional heritage management to current efforts to preserve the communication of our virtual worlds? We recognize that there are fascinating questions about the heritage of social media because our technologies and digital habitats are changing communication and relationships. We are appreciative of efforts to preserve an archive of our online presence, such as the preservation of the Twitterverse by the U.S. Library of Congress and Internet Archive's Wayback Machine. However, we are not delving into that particular heritage. That type of digital heritage, of born-digital communication, is different from digital versions of tangible heritage, such as virtual reconstructions of archaeological sites.

In *Playing with the Past*, Erik Champion (2011) discusses virtual heritage as the representation of the tangible through digital media. He is most concerned about accuracy and authenticity with the aim of educating through engaging presentations. These are laudable goals, but as Neil Silberman (2008) points out, virtual heritage cannot be an objective reconstruction, and we risk being blinded by the technology and the entertainment value of such heritage presentations. He worries about the dampening role that tourism and economic incentives to please visitors can play in the message of a virtual heritage presentation.

Instead, Silberman urges us to focus on the role of virtual heritage as a tool for historical reflection in contemporary society. He reminds us that "the value of the past is precisely to teach us new things, not only to reassure or amuse us—to offer difficult themes for public discussion and reflection, a task hardly possible when the goal is to capture a market share of recreational activities" (2008, 85). In this sense, virtual heritage and physical, tangible heritage present us with the same challenges: to learn about ourselves and our capacities through the past and the stories we tell about it; to be surprised, horrified, and delighted by those discoveries; and to be inspired to struggle for the common good.

Civic Engagement and Social Justice

Heritage workers face a challenge to broaden personal and community histories to encompass wider communities and the human family that stands to benefit from bridging connections with the past and with each other through shared history. Civic engagement is a current that runs through this book and is especially important in our discussions of service learning in higher education and the mechanisms for coming to public judgment.

We adopt the working definition of *civic engagement* from the University of Maryland's Coalition for Civic Engagement and Leadership: Steering Committee of the Coalition for Civic Engagement and Leadership (2005), which reads as follows:

> Civic engagement is acting upon a heightened sense of responsibility to one's communities. This includes a wide range of activities, including developing civic sensitivity, participation in building civil society, and benefiting the common good. Civic engagement encompasses the notions of global citizenship and interdependence. Through civic engagement, individuals —as citizens of their communities, their nations, and the world—are empowered as agents of positive social change for a more democratic world. Civic engagement involves one or more of the following:
>
> 1. Learning from others, self, and environment to develop informed perspectives on social issues;
>
> 2. Recognizing and appreciating human diversity and commonality;
>
> 3. Behaving, and working through controversy, with civility;
>
> 4. Participating actively in public life, public problem solving, and community service;
>
> 5. Assuming leadership and membership roles in organizations;
>
> 5. Developing empathy, ethics, values, and sense of social responsibility;
>
> 7. Promoting social justice locally and globally.

Civic Engagement as the Development of Social Capital

People can work individually or collectively on issues of public concern. Through both political and nonpolitical processes, people recognize that they are part of a larger social fabric (Ehrlich 2000a, vi). The goal of civic engagement is to become an active player in change, to not only work in communities but with communities, and to work toward creating a better quality of life.

Social capital, the development of networks within and between groups, is an outcome of civic engagement. The development of social networks is a way of creating cooperation between individuals and groups to obtain collective results. However, it is important to point out that social scientists use and define social capital in different ways. Some also challenge the benefits of civic engagement activities and the promotion of social capital and social justice.

Social capital is seen by many to be an essential element in addressing problems of modern society. Social networks have value as interconnection can affect individuals and groups in a positive way. The power of community and the enhancement of the democratic process have been recognized as an important part of Western civilization since the development of ancient Greece. The Greeks experimented with a form of direct democracy, whereby all citizens could be chosen to serve in government and all citizens were expected to vote. However, it should be noted that citizens included only adult males, and did not include women, children, or the enslaved. From Aristotle in the fourth century BCE to Edmund Burke in the eighteenth century, social philosophers have recognized the importance of social capital (Bowles and Gintis 2002, F419).

The ideals of social connectedness became vibrant again among the philosophers of the Renaissance era. In the nineteenth century, writers like Alexis de Tocqueville, drawing on the works of earlier scholars, described the social cohesion and connectedness that underlay the pluralist tradition in America (Ferragina 2010). In 1916, L. J. Hanifan became one of the first social scientists to refer to the importance of social capital in the form of goodwill, fellowship, mutual sympathy, and social intercourse among a group of individuals and families. In referring to a rural community, he notes:

> If he may come into contact with his neighbor, and they with other neighbors, there will be an accumulation of social capital, which may immediately satisfy his social needs and which may bear a social potentiality sufficient to the substantial improvement of living conditions in the whole community. The community as a whole will benefit by the cooperation of all its parts, while the individual will find in his associations the advantages of the help, the sympathy, and the fellowship of his neighbors (130–131).

Many of the social scientists writing at the turn of the twentieth century, including Émile Durkheim (1893), Georg Simmel (1905), and a bit later, Max Weber (1946), discussed the decline of community and connectedness as the Western world modernized and industrialized in favor of a more individual-

Figure 3.2   Exterior of the Jane Adams's Hull House on the University of Illinois, Chicago campus. (Photograph by Paul A. Shackel.)

istic society. They observed that industrialization and urbanization led to a breakdown of traditional bonds, leading to the development of anomie and alienation in society (Ferragina 2010). While social scientists were describing the increasing development of social alienation in America, social capital was at a low point and many social and community needs were not being met. Progressive-era reformers responded by creating organizations like the Salvation Army (1880), Red Cross (1881), Knights of Columbus (1882), Sierra Club (1892), Volunteers of America (1896), 4–H (1901), Goodwill Industries (1902), Big Brother (1903), Rotary (1905), Big Sister (1908), Community Chest/United Way (1913), Lions Club (1917), the League of Women Voters (1920), and the National Urban League (1920), in order to enhance social capital and provide for the needs of the underserved sectors of the community (Crowley and Skocpol 2001, 871; Gates 2002, 25; Tolbert et al. 2003, 24) (figure 3.2). Communities solved problems that might otherwise appear as classic market or state failures (Bowles and Gintis 2002, F419). Americans were able to rebuild their communities with these and other cooperative groups, and for the next several decades, social scientists continued to focus on the deterioration of community (Ferragina 2010, 76).

The term *social capital* has been used and defined in different ways by scholars. In the 1970s, Pierre Bourdieu (1977) redefined social capital in his book *Outline of a Theory of Practice*. He saw social capital as the access to resources and the access to participation in structured social organizations. According to him, social capital functions at the individual level, as individuals gain access to power through social connections. Social capital is used to produce or reproduce inequality. Bourdieu applied the term to a very different concept related to power and power building.

Robert Putnam, a professor of public policy, sees the implementation of social capital in a more collective way. According to Putnam's well-known work *Bowling Alone: The Collapse and Revival of American Community* (2000), Americans have become disengaged from the communal life of society in general, and from the responsibilities of democracy in particular. In *Bowling Alone* Putnam shows that since about 1980, Americans have increasingly become disconnected from communities and family. The decreasing access to social capital is a serious threat to both civic and personal health. He frames social capital as a broad societal measure of communal health, and distinguishes it as an attribute of collectives rather than a resource possessed by individuals. Putnam identifies two different types of social capital: bonding social capital and bridging social capital. Bonding is exclusive and homogenizing. It builds internal cohesion within groups, such as self-serving exclusive gangs and hierarchical patronage systems. Bridging acts to cross social divides and creates networks between socially heterogeneous groups. The networking of individuals and groups enhances community productivity and cohesion. Horizontal networks of individual citizens and groups that enhance community productivity and cohesion are positive social capital assets.

The Saguaro Seminar on Civic Engagement in America, an initiative of Robert Putnam's at the John F. Kennedy School of Government at Harvard University, is a project that works to expand knowledge about trust and community engagement and to develop strategies to increase that engagement. The Seminar's multi-year (1995–2000) dialogue on building bonds of civic trust is summarized in the report "BetterTogether," which is available online. The report (2000, 97) describes the blending of both kinds of social capital:

> This bridging social capital helps to forge a common ground and promote citizen responsibility and engagement...mixed forms of bridging and bonding social capital may represent the most practical way of

meeting our twin goals of greatly increasing community connectedness while multiplying our interactions with people unlike ourselves....In sum, we support all social capital strategies, as long as groups that are privileged or advantaged do not demonize those who do not or cannot belong. We seek strategies that will raise the aggregate level of trustworthiness and trust in society.

There are also those who see the promotion and development of social capital as inappropriate and as an attack on neo-liberal economic development (Fine 2001). However, the lack of social capital often leads to a rigid and unresponsive political system. In order for a modern liberal democracy to function, social capital needs to be sustained and reinforced. Attacks on social capital are often accompanied by attacks on the promotion of social justice. On the other hand, civic engagement is framed as active participation in civil society with the intention of doing good and promoting social justice.

Social justice refers to the overall fairness of the rewards and burdens in society. It can be attained through cooperative effort of citizens who believe that all persons are entitled to basic human needs, regardless of economic disparity, class, gender, race, ethnicity, citizenship, religion, age, sexual orientation, disability, or health. Some view social justice as a moral and ethical balance to less-than-effective government-sponsored legal justice. They believe that historical inequities should be addressed and corrected, and those who hold significant power should be responsible for ensuring a basic quality of life for all citizens. Michael Dodson wrote in 1993 in his first Annual Report of the Aboriginal and Torres Strait Islander Social Justice Commissioner:

> Social justice is what faces you when you get up in the morning. It is awakening in a house with an adequate water supply, cooking facilities and sanitation. It is the ability to nourish your children and send them to school where their education not only equips them for employment but reinforces their knowledge and understanding of their cultural inheritance. It is the prospect of genuine employment and good heath: a life of choices and opportunity, free from discrimination (8).

In his article "Defining Social Justice," Michael Novak (2000) argues that social justice does not belong to any political or social group, left or right of center, but rather social justice contributes to the development of a civil society, which requires working with and organizing others to accomplish works of justice. Social justice is aimed at doing good for a whole and for the good of others. "Its field of activity may be literary, scientific, religious, political, economic, cultural, athletic, and so on, across the whole spectrum of human social activities" (13).

Helaine Silverman and D. Fairchild Ruggles (2007, 17) describe how the contributing authors in their volume *Cultural Heritage and Human Rights*, "see a direct linkage between human rights and cultural heritage at the local scale, which, in turn, ultimately contributes, in the aggregate, to fulfilment of the global [justice] goal." Barbara Little (2012) explores the ways in which archaeology can contribute to the goals of the global justice movement. She argues that archaeology can examine the deep history of contemporary issues such as migration and treatment of foreigners; poverty, hunger, and subsistence; military power; and urban decay. Archaeologists can draw upon their discoveries and approaches to come up with new narratives to help improve present and future environmental and social conditions and to respond intelligently to climate change.

In this book we are using the term social justice as an umbrella term for fairness within society that covers not only political and civil rights, but also economic, social, and cultural rights. It is this latter set of rights to which we now turn.

Chapter 4

The Second Bill of Rights

Carved in the granite walls of the Franklin Delano Roosevelt Memorial are the four freedoms that he strongly supported during his presidency and made famous in his "Four Freedoms" speech as part of his Annual Message to Congress on January 6, 1941 (figure 4.1):

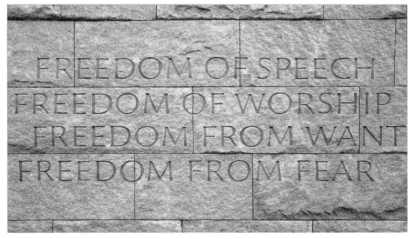

Figure 4.1   The Four Freedoms from the Second Bill of Rights, Franklin D. Roosevelt Memorial, Washington, DC. (Image courtesy of http://en.wikipedia.org/wiki/File:FDR_Memorial_wall.jpg.)

Archaeology, Heritage, and Civic Engagement, Barbara J. Little and Paul A. Shackel, p. 53–62.

- Freedom of speech
- Freedom of worship
- Freedom from want
- Freedom from fear

The first two are, of course, from the Bill of Rights. During his State of the Union address to Congress on January 11, 1944, Roosevelt proposed what he called an economic bill of rights (table 4.1). This list of proposed rights has become known as the Second Bill of Rights and supplements the civil and political rights detailed in the first ten amendments to the U.S. Constitution (Kloppenberg 2006, 509). Cass Sunstein (2004) observes that Roosevelt's Second Bill of Rights is largely unknown to most people and suggests it should be reclaimed by the citizens of the United States.

During his first campaign for president, Roosevelt began speaking about the need in the United States for economic and social rights. While he spent the next dozen years advocating for those rights, it was not until his January 11, 1944, State of the Union Address to Congress that he fully conceptualized and expressed his ideas (Democratic Underground 2013). While many critics say the speech was far from elegant, and it has been largely lost, overshadowed in the memory of the war, Sunstein (2004, B9) suggests that it has a strong claim to being the "greatest speech of the 20th century" for what it proposed.

In his State of the Union Address in January 1944, Roosevelt observed that the Bill of Rights gave U.S. citizens some inalienable political rights. However, he believed that these basic rights needed to be expanded. Roosevelt claimed that, "We have come to a clear realization of the fact that true individual freedom cannot exist without economic security and independence." He argued that while the war was winding down in Europe, the United States must invest in security. This included physical security, economic security, social security, and moral security. This security would also enable greater democracy building in the United States and support equality in the pursuit of happiness. He explained, "Essential to peace is a decent standard of living for all individual men and women and children in all Nations. Freedom from fear is eternally linked with freedom from want". He later insisted, "We cannot be content, no matter how high that general standard of living may be, if some fraction of our people—whether it be one-third or one-fifth or one-tenth—is ill-fed, ill-clothed, ill-housed, and insecure" (Roosevelt 1944). He proposed that the Second Bill of Rights should be established for all—regardless of station, race, or creed.

TABLE 4.1: ROOSEVELT'S ECONOMIC BILL OF RIGHTS

Excerpted from Franklin D. Roosevelt's State of the Union Message to Congress, January 11, 1944, available at http://www.fdrlibrary.marist.edu/archives/address_text.html.

The one supreme objective for the future, which we discussed for each Nation individually, and for all the United Nations, can be summed up in one word: Security.

And that means not only physical security which provides safety from attacks by aggressors. It means also economic security, social security, moral security—in a family of Nations.

…Freedom from fear is eternally linked with freedom from want.

…This Republic had its beginning, and grew to its present strength, under the protection of certain inalienable political rights—among them the right of free speech, free press, free worship, trial by jury, freedom from unreasonable searches and seizures. They were our rights to life and liberty.

As our Nation has grown in size and stature, however—as our industrial economy expanded—these political rights proved inadequate to assure us equality in the pursuit of happiness.

We have come to a clear realization of the fact that true individual freedom cannot exist without economic security and independence. "Necessitous men are not free men." People who are hungry and out of a job are the stuff of which dictatorships are made.

In our day these economic truths have become accepted as self-evident. We have accepted, so to speak, a second Bill of Rights under which a new basis of security and prosperity can be established for all regardless of station, race, or creed.

Among these are:

The right to a useful and remunerative job in the industries or shops or farms or mines of the Nation;

The right to earn enough to provide adequate food and clothing and recreation;

The right of every farmer to raise and sell his products at a return which will give him and his family a decent living;

The right of every businessman, large and small, to trade in an atmosphere of freedom from unfair competition and domination by monopolies at home or abroad;

The right of every family to a decent home;

The right to adequate medical care and the opportunity to achieve and enjoy good health;

The right to adequate protection from the economic fears of old age, sickness, accident, and unemployment;

The right to a good education.

All of these rights spell security. And after this war is won we must be prepared to move forward, in the implementation of these rights, to new goals of human happiness and well-being.

America's own rightful place in the world depends in large part upon how fully these and similar rights have been carried into practice for our citizens. For unless there is security here at home there cannot be lasting peace in the world.

…Each and every one of us has a solemn obligation under God to serve this Nation in its most critical hour—to keep this Nation great—to make this Nation greater in a better world.

The Roosevelt administration made progress toward many of these rights through executive orders and by pushing Congress to enact legislation such as the Social Security Act of 1935. He also sponsored the development of several agencies that produced jobs for the working class, labor protection laws and the right for workers to organize into unions, the federal minimum wage, antitrust policies, and the GI Bill of Rights (Democratic Underground 2013).

The Second Bill of Rights was greeted with horror by those who resisted the New Deal, and it was minimized in the United States, buried in the rhetoric of the early Cold War. While Franklin Roosevelt died fifteen months after delivering his address, Eleanor Roosevelt, who played a major role in developing the Universal Declaration of Human Rights, incorporated many of these ideas into that document, which was adopted by the United Nations (UN) in 1948. These rights laid the foundation for additional international covenants. The UN General Assembly adopted the International Covenant on Economic, Social and Cultural Rights (ICESCR) on December 16, 1966, and went into effect in 1976. The International Covenant on Civil and Political Rights (ICCPR) was also adopted the same day and went into effect ten years later. At the time of writing this book, there are 161 parties to the ICESCR—member states that have ratified, acceded to, or succeeded to it. Seventy members have signed it, but not all of them have also ratified it. The United States signed the ICESCR in 1977, but has not ratified it. The United States signed the ICCPR in 1977, and ratified it in 1992 (UN 2013).

The ideas in the Second Bill of Rights are found in many of the newer constitutions of countries such as Finland, Spain, Ukraine, Romania, Syria, Bulgaria, Hungary, Russia, and Peru. Article XIV of the interim Iraqi constitution, celebrated in the United States by the second Bush administration, states that, "the individual has the right to security, education, health care, and social security" (Kloppenberg 2006, 511; Sunstein 2004, B10). Sunstein (2004) points out that in the United States these "rights" can be developed through reinterpretation of the Constitution by the courts. They can also be developed through citizens when they reach general consensus as to what constitutes a "right." This latter point is important because it recognizes that claiming of rights is an emergent process and one that can be driven by people, not only by governments. We are seeing this emergence internationally, particularly in regard to definitions of cultural rights.

In the past few decades, the international community has shown increasing interest in the idea of economic, social, and cultural (ESC) rights. These

ESC rights have only been vaguely defined, but the movement toward their serious consideration is worldwide. Ideas about rights are evolving, especially in the context of globalization. There has not been nearly as much in-depth discussion or court proceedings intended to define and secure ESC rights as there has been for civil and political rights (Holder 2008).

Silverman and Ruggles (2007) remark that heritage has an uneasy place in the concept of universal human rights because of the apparent inherent conflict between universal rights and individual rights, but they call for heritage to rank as an essential component of human rights. They note that human rights and cultural heritage may overlap and conflict. Such conflict may occur: in terms of indigenous rights (which are often articulated in resistance to national identity), war and other violence (political, ethnic, religious), access to and exclusion from shared sacred sites, the impact of economic development on cultural heritage of local populations, memory and forgetting, and intellectual property rights (6–7).

The Emergent Nature of Cultural Rights

Cultural rights are recognized as underdeveloped legally, in part because they are different from other rights. Professor of International Law and Human Rights Francesco Francioni (2008) explains that other rights come from human similarities, from shared human dignity, but culture is what is unique and different among peoples. He notes how firmly culture is connected with heritage: "The term 'cultural heritage' today represents the totality of cultural objects, traditions, knowledge and skills that a given nation or community has inherited by way of the learning process from previous generations and which provides its sense of identity to be transmitted to subsequent generations" (6).

Internationally, the term *heritage* was first adopted with the 1972 UNESCO Convention concerning the Protection of the World Cultural and Natural Heritage. The meaning of the term expanded beyond property to include practice and beyond the tangible to include the intangible with subsequent conventions and charters. Francioni (2008, 7) argues that, "This incremental expansion of the concept of cultural heritage in the practice of international law has had the consequence of strengthening the conceptual link between heritage and cultural rights."

The political paradigm shifted internationally with the UNESCO Universal Declaration on Cultural Diversity in 2001. Patrice Meyer-Bisch (2013), founder of the l'Observatoire de la diversité et des droits culturels in France, writes that this paradigm change has brought cultural rights forward in international considerations of human rights. The most pressing issue is the need to clarify the relationship between universal human rights and ideas about cultural relativism. He finds such clarification necessary in order to prevent nations from claiming cultural relativism as a pretext for denying certain universal human rights. Specifically, he emphasizes the need to *strengthen indivisibility and interdependence*:

> The subject is unconditionally an individual person, but in order to fulfill its rights, it may claim membership in one or many communities, groups or organized collectivities. A community may be a precious space, even a necessary one, to exercise rights, freedoms and responsibilities, and it therefore deserves protection: it allows one to experience transmission, sharing, reciprocity and the confrontation of knowledge. But a community only has conditional legitimacy, to the extent in which it promotes human rights.

Contributors to the volume *Cultural Diversity, Heritage and Human Rights: Intersections in Theory and Practice* (Langfield et al. 2010) aim to link the three concepts suggested by the book's title—conserving cultural heritage, maintaining cultural diversity, and enforcing human rights. The book's editors identify several key dilemmas critical to cultural heritage theory and practice:

> How are the cultural rights of ethnic minority groups best protected? Is the commodification of their cultures through cultural tourism a problem that requires a policy response? How do we deal with situations where local communities prefer to achieve higher standards of living by rejecting tradition and modernizing their cultures? How do we deal in practice with situations where cultural heritage is used by powerful actors, both domestic and external, to obtain political goals that are essentially unrelated to heritage conservation? How do we respond as professionals to instances where various claims to cultural practices based on human rights are in conflict with each other? (15–16).

The editors of *Cultural Diversity, Heritage and Human Rights* writing in the first chapter (Logan et al. 2010) bemoan the lack of connection between the UNESCO World Heritage program and human rights. However, we want to emphasize that the International Coalition of Sites of Conscience has stepped in with a non-governmental approach to making the connection between heritage and human rights. Their member sites are committed to using historic sites, museums, and cultural institutions as sites of conscience where dialogue can happen around critical and pressing human rights issues. We discuss the coalition's work a little later and offer an approach to making such connections in our final chapter.

Silencing Heritage: Cultural Violence in Arizona

In light of the Four Freedoms and the emerging ESC rights that support them, we want to consider a current situation in the United States where cultural rights are under attack. In May 2010, the governor of Arizona signed a bill that banned ethnic studies classes in public schools. This legislation known as Arizona House Bill 2281 and codified in Arizona Revised Statutes (A.R.S.) § 15-111, 15-112) states:

> 15-111. Declaration of policy
> The legislature finds and declares that public school pupils should be taught to treat and value each other as individuals and not be taught to resent or hate other races or classes of people.
>
> 15-112. Prohibited courses and classes; enforcement
> A.   A school district or charter school in this state shall not include in its program of instruction any courses or classes that include any of the following:
> 1. Promote the overthrow of the United States government.
> 2. Promote resentment toward a race or class of people.
> 3. Are designed primarily for pupils of a particular ethnic group.
> 4. Advocate ethnic solidarity instead of the treatment of pupils as individuals.

The law was written in response to a program in the Tucson Unified School District on Mexican American history and culture (figure 4.2). Proponents of and participants in that program argue that it not only taught U.S. history but also that it encouraged students to stay in school (Creative News Group 2013).

The *Christian Science Monitor* reported in May 2010 that, "A group of United Nations human rights experts expressed concern earlier this week about both the immigration and ethnic studies laws in Arizona. Everyone has

Figure 4.2   The Bullion Plaza Cultural Center and Museum, formerly the Bullion Plaza School, in Miami, Arizona. Serving as a grammar school from 1923 to 1994, the school was operated as the town's "Mexican" school, reflecting the segregation pattern found in many Arizona communities. The school was desegregated in the 1950–1951 school year. (Image courtesy of Globe Miami Times). For more information see: www.nps.gov/history/nr/feature/hispanic/2008/bullion_plaza_school.htm and https://www.facebook.com/bullion.plaza.

the right to seek and develop cultural knowledge and to know and understand his or her own culture" (quoted in Khadaroo 2010).

In March of 2013, Judge Wallace Tashima of the United States Court of Appeals for the Ninth Circuit upheld most of the law. Item three concerning classes designed for particular ethnic groups was ruled unconstitutionally vague. In his ruling, Tashima found that the law and public discussion about it: "may be viewed to spark suspicion that the Latino population has been improperly targeted....This single-minded focus on terminating the [Mexican American studies] program, along with Horne's decision not to issue findings against other ethnic studies programs, is at least suggestive of discriminatory intent" [quoted in Carcamo 2013].

The *Los Angeles Times* reported that even though Judge Tashima ruled that the law raised serious concern that it would "chill the teaching of legitimate and objective ethnic studies courses," the state's attorney general Tom Horne, who wrote the law, declared the ruling a "victory for ensuring that public education is not held captive to radical, political elements and that students treat each other as individuals—not on the basis of the race they were born into" (quoted in Carcamo 2013).

This kind of language from the attorney general is remarkable for its logical gymnastics. It attempts to label teachers of Mexican American studies as radical and political while implying a high moral ground for his own actions, amplified into a statewide ban on the rights of some to learn history relevant to current identity. There are many battle lines being drawn in Arizona between citizen and immigrant and the struggles take place not just along the Mexican-U.S. border. All forms of violence are occurring: direct, structural, and cultural. In this particular case the cultural violence has become much more explicit than usual. The tools include not only racial and ethnic categories, but also basic concepts supporting the very idea of personhood and identity. The Arizona law attacks the very concept that people have a right to maintain an identity and a culture. The law privileges a focus on the individual at the expense of recognition of collective identity as part of a group or cultural heritage.

The Arizona law links heritage consciousness to both fostering resentment, presumably by Latinos against "whites," and to the threat of treason and the overthrow of the U.S. government. Apparently the nation would be threatened when people understand what happened in the past. Is there actual danger there? In an article entitled, "The new threat to history," Eric Hobsbawm (1993, 62–64) wrote, "As poppies are the raw material of heroin addiction, history is the raw material for nationalist or ethnic or fundamentalist ideologies. Heritage is an essential, perhaps the essential, element in these ideologies." Of course, heritage is a powerful force, and though it is used by people in a variety of ways, heritage does not operate in a vacuum. It is thoroughly integrated into the social, political and economic structures that label, target, and do violence to certain groups of people while simultaneously pretending that only individuals matter.

Chapter 5

Public Judgment

The Persistence and Changeability of Narrative

There is a stubbornness to heritage stories that flummoxes scholars. The distance between myth and truth or between heritage and history sometimes appears to be unbridgeable. In his book, *A Voyage Long and Strange: On the Trail of Vikings, Conquistadors, Lost Colonists, and other Adventurers in Early America,* the writer Tony Horwitz explores heritage stories that are integral to Americans' sense of the past. Horwitz (2008, 387) quotes a conversation he had with Harvard's Reverend Peter Gomes about the Pilgrims and Plymouth. Gomes said, "Myth is more important than history. History is arbitrary, a collection of facts. Myth we choose, we create, we perpetuate....The story here may not be correct, but it transcends truth. It's like religion—beyond facts. Myth trumps fact, always does, always will." Horwitz's own musings after researching his book on the European explorations that took place between Columbus's voyages and the founding of Jamestown and Plymouth in what is now the United States suggest a similar finding. As he stands before Plymouth Rock in Plymouth, Massachusetts, Horwitz writes, "I could chase after facts across early America, uncover hidden or forgotten "truths," explode fantasies about the country's founding. But in the end it made little difference. Myth remained intact, as stubbornly embedded as the lump of granite in the pit before me" (388).

And yet, stories about the past do change. Civil rights movements have changed some stories and added others to the American repertoire. Scholarship that adds the hidden or erased histories of minorities to "mainstream" history is crucial in this regard and is why research focused on underrepresented groups continues to be an essential ingredient in struggles for equality. Relationships within society and the heritage stories that support them change together, although sometimes very slowly. Intentional effort is necessary to raise consciousness, work through meanings, and change cultural narratives, expectations, and reality.

When engaging any constituency with heritage issues, it may well be the case that responsible public judgment has not yet formed around particular issues. We might expect this especially when proposing new ways of using heritage to work toward justice for traditionally marginalized or erased groups. For example, ideas that support the status quo of privilege based on whiteness may be deeply embedded in a community and, perhaps, even tacitly embraced and celebrated. Such ideas become dysfunctional in a public sphere that has broadened to claim support for the rights of all people, but new responsible ways to deal with the issues may not yet have developed.

Part of the struggle and staying power of institutional racism and other persistent bigotries is how embedded they are in our heritage stories about ourselves and who we are. These are the hidden structures we alluded to in the introduction when we introduced Eric Gable's writing and his insight into the white identity message at Monticello, and Terrance Weik's discussion of the marginalization of the freedom struggles of African Americans and others.

Democracy, Public Judgment, and Heritage

Public judgment and public opinion are not the same thing. Opinions are often raw, unstable, or unexamined, especially for their consequences. Public judgment may take a long time to form. It starts with raising consciousness and it forms through intentional cognitive effort, working through necessary changes in attitude and action.

Daniel Yankelovich has been widely influential in the work of engaging citizens in complex issues. In *Coming to Public Judgment: Making Democracy Work in a Complex World* (1991) he described the development of the kind of responsible public judgment necessary for democracy to function, and contrasted it with mass opinion, which is often fickle and characterized by top-of-the-mind responses.

Yankelovich (1991, 2010) argues that people advance through three distinct stages before they form politically meaningful judgments about public issues. The first stage is "consciousness raising" when people become aware of an issue and start to take it seriously. The second stage is "working through" when the need for change starts to become apparent and trade-offs come into focus. This is a difficult and emotionally charged stage where people struggle to reconcile their values with the issues. This stage can take a very long time as Yankelovich (2010, 17) notes: "The time required for people to come to sound judgment on complex, emotion-laden issues depends on the issue and varies enormously. Some issues require only months to complete the learning curve to reach sound public judgment; other issues take decades or even centuries (e.g., slavery or women's rights)." To reach sound public judgment, this "working through" requires confronting wishful thinking. The third stage is "resolution" that arrives at a course of action. Public judgment implies that people have worked through emotional and intellectual issues and are prepared to accept the consequences of their actions.

Daniel Yankelovich and Will Friedman (2010) take stock of public judgment today with the aim of reinventing the public process of solving problems. Some challenges are long-standing, such as the human propensity for wishful thinking and looking for easy answers without consequences. Some challenges are created or stoked by the way we live today, with technology and media that make it very easy to follow only information channels that reinforce our own ideas and allow us to avoid the cognitive dissonance of ideas, opinions, and experience that do not match our own but might encourage us to question our beliefs.

Delving into the implications of these models of public judgment is useful for heritage work because they provide important insights about the roles of experts and the public in a democracy and, perhaps more importantly, provide insights into the relative importance of information, emotion, and values in decision making. Values and emotion, maybe more so than factual information, play central roles in heritage.

Yankelovich and Friedman (2010) summarize three results from their analysis of decades of data. First, media reporting is based on assumptions that bear little resemblance to the ways in which people actually think. The assumption that people simply need more or more accurate information to make informed and well-reasoned decisions is not supported by research. Facts and increased information play only a minor role in the public's learning curve. Second, in the decades since the publication of *Coming to Public Judgment*, citizen engagement workers have developed and implemented new methods to help people consider and come to judgment on complex and critical issues. Many of these new methods are based on the process of dialogue, which we discuss later in this chapter. Using them can help speed up the often lengthy process of working through issues. Third, although people are demanding a larger role in political decision making, there is little appreciation for the difference between raw opinion and considered public judgment. Therefore, lots of time and energy is spent on generating and influencing public opinion but little on increasing the quality of public judgment. Yankelovich and Friedman fault the media for clinging to outmoded ideas, elites for their self-interest and indifference to the public, and the academy for being oblivious. The current dynamic, then, appears to leave out not only many different public voices, but also relevant voices of experts, because neither kind of voice is able to be heard by the other.

Are workers in heritage fields elitist or oblivious in ways that might make it difficult for us to invest in the working through of public judgment? The worldviews and narrative styles of experts who think of themselves as apart from the public are part of the problem. One of the forces working against sounder public judgment is the persistent gap between scientists and technical experts and the general public due to differing worldviews and values (Yankelovich 2010). Scientists continually call for greater scientific literacy without recognizing their own responsibility for the lack of mutually intelligible communication.

The contrasts between science and public life will remind archaeologists of characterizations of positivism. Scientists expect the world to be rational, lawful, and orderly while public life is irrational, discontinuous, and disorderly. The long view and international perspective of scientific research and verification bumps up against the general public's needs for immediate solutions to urgent problems. Policymakers do not believe that they can afford to wait for rational analysis to come up with solutions. The public tends not to be comfortable with the concept of probabilities, which is integral to scientific understanding, rather it wants certainties. In this situation, recognition of the social, political, and cultural context of our work are necessary to engage thoroughly and ethically with the public.

Insights from the work of Yankelovich and of colleagues in civic engagement and dialogue can be combined with those from the field of rhetoric, which along with the social sciences, took a public turn in the 1980s. Our own heritage fields are working through the dilemmas posed by the developments in practice and theory that make engagement with the public necessary. We have struggled with the question of what roles experts ought to play in community-based or community-driven collaboration. In some cases, highly educated and accomplished experts become so worried about how their expertise might control outcomes that they remove their expertise with the intention to allow the community to come to its own decision. We believe that this is a counterproductive strategy that not only denies the value of expertise to the community, but also negates the power of the community to engage thoroughly with and participate in whatever field of expertise is involved. Expertise is not interference when it is offered ethically and in a spirit of collaboration. Experts are legitimate stakeholders and expertise is often essential to good decision making.

How can heritage play a role in the public work of making meaning and values? How can heritage help us understand the consequences of the choices we make? Think about a shift in perception and policy at the level of a local house museum. We draw our generalization from a case in Lexington, Kentucky (Stahlgren 2012). The elites in charge are invested—even unconsciously—in a long-standing heritage story about white plantation owners and their visible material wealth. The experts (archaeologists in this case) have recent scholarship and training that encourage an ethical stance explicitly promoting inclusion. The experts make proposals to the elites based not only on the value of information and science as an elite value but also invoking different values, based on perceptions about race, fairness, and inclusion. The proposal is to tell the story of enslaved African Americans at the plantation site. Incorporating that material led to an outcome well beyond the simple addition of information, and changed relationships on site and in the city.

The heritage fields, along with the social sciences in general, took a public turn in the 1980s as did the field of rhetoric. Rhetoricians work in theorizing how publics and public spheres are constructed. M. Lane Bruner (2010, 56) identifies some emerging questions in the field of rhetoric that connect in interesting ways with emerging issues in the heritage professions:

- What are the interrelationships among our real and imagined worlds?

- How does the construction of public memory impact the health of the state?…

- What, in sum, is the relationship between identity construction and the healthy state?

The hegemonic public, which claims mainstream status, always creates unmet demands. As Bruner explains the process, isolated demands can be repressed, ignored, or integrated into the hegemonic system. However, when unmet demands coalesce, they form a counterpublic with enough force to transform the hegemonic public, which in turn creates unmet demands and so the process continues. A sick state is characterized by repressed critique, while a healthy state has enough active public spheres to encourage counterpublics and constant critique.

Bruner is interested in constructing the healthiest possible publics and states. He sees a direct relationship between the quality of human communication and the healthy state, and he identifies perceptions about the past as crucial to such health. When perceived and real history do not match in the hegemonic public, the state more easily becomes sick. Bruner asks: "What role can communication scholars play in alleviating this world-historical problem of the persistent distance between fact and opinion, between knowledge and belief, and between the unfolding of history and its complex causes and the way that history is characterized and interpreted?" (69).

This question is one that heritage workers can usefully ask themselves. What is our role in bridging these divides? In supporting a healthy public and a healthy state?

It is not necessary to be Pollyannaish about democracy to believe in the power of deliberative democracy through dialogue to get to reasoned and widely acceptable actions to define and solve problems. Democracy itself does not guarantee any particular outcomes, but it is the working model for how current American society operates and supports the model of dialogue that feeds the working through stage of public judgment. We believe that it is necessary to balance a healthy skepticism about the powers of democracy to solve long-term problems with a healthy optimism about the power of intentional dialogue in public spheres to work through such problems. This balance may require that people give up short-term gains.

Citizens in a democracy need learned skills for the working through stage of coming to public judgment. In the United States, some of the many organizations supporting civic engagement and public judgment are Public Agenda, the National Issues Forum, the Center for Information and Research on Civic

Learning and Engagement (CIRCLE), and Viewpoint Learning. They offer materials and guidance for framing critical and pressing issues such as health care, energy and climate change, education, and immigration and ethnic tensions.

By itself, or framed in the specific mundane terms of compliance with a legal requirement, heritage may pale in comparison to perceived emergencies. However, it is integral to values, perception, identity, and relationships with others, whoever the others may be. Because heritage is implicated in structural and cultural violence, it is a critical issue of our day. Part of a heritage-focused approach to problem solving would highlight how ordinary citizens, individually and collectively, have identified and solved problems and how their approaches and solutions were situated in social, psychological, emotional, political, and historical settings.

The middle stage of working through, essential to public judgment is where dialogue comes in. Dialogue in this practice of working through is not just conversation and, again, Yankelovich (1999) is an able guide. While debate is based on the assumption that there is a right answer and the debater has it, dialogue assumes that many people have pieces of the right answer and must come together to craft a solution. Dialogue supports respect for differing points of view and nurtures civility. Three criteria are essential to dialogue:

1. equality and an absence of coercion

2. empathetic listening

3. bringing assumptions—our deeply held beliefs—out into the open fearlessly

Meeting those conditions is not easy; it requires mutual trust, which can take enormous effort and emotional investment to build. Trust and listening are essential to true collaboration, a point to which we now turn.

Chapter 6

Collaboration

Trending Toward Collaboration

Collaboration is an increasingly central concept in heritage fields. Working effectively across disciplinary boundaries, across structural boundaries, and with local or descendant communities requires collaboration. In archaeology, the shifting meanings of collaboration and what it entails and the evolving reasons for doing it are mirrored in the structure of the book *Cross-Cultural Collaboration: Native Peoples and Archaeology in the Northeastern United States* (Kerber 2006). Two thirds of the book concerns collaboration in terms of regulatory compliance while the last part concerns voluntary collaboration. Voluntary work is more likely to be fully collaborative. Jordan Kerber, the book's editor, attributes the increase in collaboration to both the enactment of the Native American Graves Protection and Repatriation Act (NAGPRA) in 1990 and the 1992 amendments to the National Historic Preservation Act (NHPA). Legal and regulatory requirements for consultation have forced interactions that were not consistently taking place beforehand. Most thoughtful discussions of collaboration come to conclusions similar to those Kerber (2006, xxx) describes: "collaboration between Native Americans and archaeologists is valuable to both groups, and that there is not one way or formula to ensure successful collaboration. Improving communication, sharing power and control as equal partners, and maintaining mutual respect are key ingredients."

Archaeology has struggled to deal with the new realities brought about by these laws and by generations of pressure by American Indians. Chip Colwell-

Chanthaphonh and T. J. Ferguson (2008) offer the model of a collaborative continuum to frame our understanding of the relationships among different approaches to collaboration. They identify collaboration as an art and a practice rather than a set process. They discuss it as a continuum that can be characterized as running from *resistance* to *participation* to *collaboration*. In this framework, the descendant stakeholder community is self-defined by those who link themselves socially, politically, or economically to the past, rather than just those relying on biological connections (10–11).

At the low (resistance) end of the continuum, resistance can arise from forced collaboration, which may result in no real collaboration at all. In that situation those involved in a project develop their goals in opposition to each other; they keep information secret and there is no stakeholder involvement and no voice for stakeholders. There is no mutual support and the needs of others are not adequately considered.

Approximately halfway along the continuum, in the participation stage, the parties involved develop their goals independently but they disclose information. There is limited stakeholder involvement with some voice for stakeholders. Participants solicit support and the needs of most parties are mostly met.

In full collaboration, there is genuine synergy. Participants develop their goals jointly and information flows freely. There is full stakeholder involvement and a full voice for stakeholders. Mutual support is tacit, and the needs of all parties are realized.

At the resistance end of the continuum, power comes through conflict. Bonding social capital can form among each of the resisting parties, fueled by opposition to the other side. At the other end, during collaboration power comes through synergy. This is where bridging social capital is likely to form, fueled by mutual needs and goals. We must maintain an awareness of power relationships in any consideration of collaboration, not only because of the normal dynamics of human interaction, but also because of the rootedness of Western sciences and practices in colonialism.

Colwell-Chanthaphonh and Ferguson (2008, 6) refer to the "persistent gene" of colonialism within archaeology, emphasizing that archaeologists need to be conscious of this past, acknowledge it, and let it influence the moral foundations of a new practice. In spite of this history, they observe that collaboration can help to build an environment of reciprocity, mutual respect, and multiple modes of knowledge production. Collaboration is challenging and it pushes the field of archaeology to expand its reach outside of the disci-

Figure 6.1   Zuni cultural advisors, Octavius Seowtewa and John Bowannie, identify an ancient shrine with archaeologist Sarah Herr during a collaborative research project in Arizona. (Image courtesy of Chip Colwell-Chanthaphonh.)

pline by including and benefiting not just other scholars, but Native communities as well (figure 6.1). It takes personal introspection and development to define best practices for collaboration, negotiating the differing needs of the researcher with the needs of the community (Nicholas et al. 2008).

NAGPRA's Legislative Impetus for Collaboration

Although some professional archaeologists have long recognized legitimate interests of Native Americans and worked with tribes, such widespread acknowledgment was forced by the passage of NAGPRA in 1990 (see especially Swidler et al. 1997; Watkins 2000). Civil rights movements in the 1950s and 1960s included the American Indian Movement (AIM) and the genesis of Native critiques of archaeology. However, Native Americans have been asserting their interest in ancestral lands and burials for centuries and in protection of the archaeologically defined past at least since the beginnings of professional archaeology.

Joe Watkins (2000) traces the increase in Native American protests against archaeologists to the publication in 1969 of Vine Deloria Jr.'s *Custer Died for Your Sins: An Indian Manifesto*. Until the 1960s, the mainstream field of archaeology, coincident with the federal government, effectively silenced the voices of Native Americans (White Deer 2000). Twenty years of protest, pressure, and lobbying eventually led to Congressional passage of NAGPRA in 1990 to provide for the repatriation of Native American, Native Hawaiian, and Native Alaskan human remains and objects of cultural patrimony that are held by federal agencies or museums that receive federal funds.

The relationship between anthropologists and Native Americans has changed significantly as a result of the passage of NAGPRA. The law acknowledges human rights by requiring repatriation of artifacts and human remains. A new body of literature written before and after the passing of NAGPRA by both American Indians and non-Indians discusses the development of a new relationship between Indians and archaeologists (Adams 1984; Anawak 1989; Echo-Hawk 2000; Ferguson 1984; Handsman and Richmond 1995; McGuire 1997; Mason 2000; Swidler et al. 1997; Watkins 2000). This new relationship has forced archaeologists to be reflexive, to recognize the political nature of archaeology, to acknowledge and incorporate alternative perceptions of the past, and to view science as not necessarily superior or more legitimate than oral history (Ferguson 1996).

Archaeologists, Native American and other descendants, and local communities are continuing to figure out ways to work effectively together to move closer to the ideal end of the collaborative continuum. Many archaeologists thought that their rights as scientists to objectively study human remains and material culture were being taken away with the passing of NAGPRA.

Those in opposition to NAGPRA believed that Western science and the traditional beliefs of Native Americans were irreconcilable. They saw NAGPRA as a political means of attacking and superseding their scientific stance with a religious one. Others have come to see NAGPRA as an opportunity to be more inclusive by acknowledging tribal views of the archaeological record. The law forced archaeologists to deconstruct the way they study indigenous heritage and work with indigenous people. NAGPRA encourages bringing Indian communities into the scholarship as active participants rather than objects to be studied. Repatriation has meant that scholars need to listen to the wishes of community members and include the stories of descendants in archaeological reporting. For Dorothy Lippert (2008), survival is an underlying theme in repatriation that returns humanity to Native American ancestors. The process also marks the end of archaeology as ahistorical and apolitical, while it enriches archaeological investigations with fuller evidence and meaning.

Lippert (2008, 126) advises us that silencing anyone's view is not in everyone's best interest: "We need not silence one another, ignore one another, or talk all at once. What is important is that we listen to one another and respect our different dialogues." She offers storytelling as common ground, as one way to connect, to listen to others ideas about heritage, history, and meaning.

Collaboration requires the active listening engendered by storytelling. While there is no cookbook for successful collaboration, there are common hallmarks and principles. George Nicholas and others (2008, 293) summarize key elements from several successful projects. Each success integrates vision, parity, responsibility, and representation. Best practices still need to be worked out in the research design of each project, but they identify five hallmarks:

1. a sense of personal satisfaction by those engaged,

2. the project is recognized as being of value (immediate and/or deferred) to community in terms of both tangible and intangible results,

3. the project facilitates subsequent interactions with the community by other researchers,

4. the collaboration is viewed as profitable to participants and the larger community,

5. there is a commitment to a long-term relationship between the researchers and the community (293).

In their experience: "Collaboration…entails mutual respect, meaningful dialogue, a long-term commitment of time and expanding 'research' to embrace processes and objectives that may not be perceived as conducive to the production and dissemination of scientific knowledge" (273).

We have focused our attention on a small sample of the collaboration literature in archaeology, but certainly collaboration is essential to any of the heritage fields and indeed any practice working toward civic engagement with true two-way communication and cooperation. Such civic engagement would fall toward the full collaboration end of the collaborative continuum. In a project to identify successful civic engagement in the National Park Service, Molly Russell (2011) interviewed project directors from a variety of fields, from resource management to law enforcement to interpretation, and identified sets of principles shared among selected projects judged to be successful by both the agency and the public participants. Russell extracted both core and secondary principles (figure 6.2). The latter are avenues by which core principles can be achieved, and while such principles are common, they are not universal. These secondary principles include 1) diversity of opinion, 2) understanding communities, 3) open communication, and 4) transparency. The secondary principles support three core principles that appeared to be

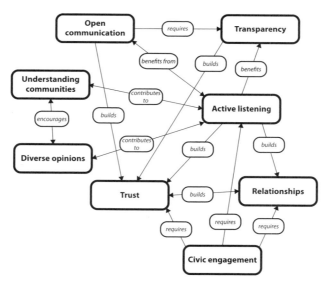

Figure 6.2   Civic Engagement Web. (Adapted from Russell 2011. Image courtesy of Molly Russell.)

essential for the success of the case studies analyzed. These core principles include 1) trust, 2) relationships, and 3) active listening. These core principles are not at all surprising, but as simple as they are, it is neither easy nor quick to achieve relationships based on trust with genuine, responsive communication that comes through active listening.

The hallmarks and principles of civic engagement have ethical implications. Because relationships between the collaborating participants depend on the participants' personal characters, Colwell-Chanthaphonh and Ferguson (2004) promote "virtue ethics" as the ethical framework that best serves collaboration. Trust is one of the core principles and trustworthiness one of the central virtues to effective collaboration. There are a variety of approaches recognized to guide ethical decision making, including those based on utility, rights, fairness, common good, as well as on virtue. Various archaeologies seek to change mainstream practice and each of them seek to be ethical. A utilitarian approach evaluates options for action according to judgments about doing the most good and least harm. An approach based on rights seeks to best respect the rights of all stakeholders. In a fairness approach, treating stakeholders equitably is most important. The common-good approach seeks to serve the community as a whole. The virtue approach seeks to meet one's own ethical standard to be the person one wants to be. Ethical decision making often considers each of the approaches and is likely to take several into account (Markkula Center for Applied Ethics 2013).

Given the nature of heritage as a meaningful component of identity, the heritage professions need to be especially attuned to listening, to dialogue, to a public "working through," and to different, often constantly changing, voices. A growing attention to a values-based approach to heritage management recognizes that there must be bridges and common ground between professionals and community. We have passed the tipping point; there is no way back to a heritage practice that operates as an expert-only domain independent of interested stakeholders.

Laws and regulations clearly have fundamental impacts on the ways in which practitioners practice. Those legal parameters can change in response to relentless public pressure often applied over a very long time. Practice also changes in response to reinterpretation of regulation, refocusing on underutilized sections of a law through public pressure, the issuance of new guidelines and policy, or on-the-ground responses to larger trends. Compliance with laws, such as NAGPRA, requires consultation and public involvement, but not necessarily the power sharing or multidirectional collaboration of civic engagement and participatory governance. The trend is toward greater true collaboration, but it is worth asking whether new laws or regulation are necessary. Can the current U.S. system be used to encourage and support increasingly collaborative and civically engaged heritage management?

Values-Based Heritage Management

Discussions of values-based management always refer to the *Burra Charter: The Australia ICOMOS Charter for Places of Cultural Significance, 2013*. Adopted by the Australian national committee of ICOMOS (International Council on Monuments and Sites), this charter is clear about involving people in the process, particularly that of identifying the cultural significance of places. Observing that analysis of value or significance is basic to every aspect of cultural heritage management, Kate Clark (2005, 328) has argued that: "It is vital that archaeologists become more aware of value-led planning as a powerful tool for sustaining cultural heritage in the long term. If we are to pass sites on to future generations, we need to recognize that management involves multiple values, different perspectives to our own, and genuine engagement with stakeholders and their concerns."

The *Burra Charter* recognizes the following types of cultural significance and allows flexibility to recognize more precise categories for particular places.

- Aesthetic value
- Historic value
- Scientific value
- Social value
- Spiritual value

How do these compare to the significance criteria for the U.S. National Register of Historic Places, established as a result of the NHPA? The four criteria for sites, buildings, structures, districts and objects are:

a. that are associated with events that have made a significant contribution to the broad patterns of our history;

b. that are associated with the lives of persons significant in our past;

c. that embody the distinctive characteristics of a type, period, or method of construction, or that represent the work of a master, or that possess high artistic values, or that represent a significant and distinguishable entity whose components may lack individual distinction;

d. that have yielded, or may be likely to yield, information important in prehistory or history.

Both (a) and (b) compare with the *Burra Charter*'s historic value, (c) with aesthetic value, and (d) with scientific value. There are no specific analogues to social or spiritual value, but the 1992 amendments to NHPA Section 101(d)(6)(A) explicitly state that "Properties of traditional religious and cultural importance to an Indian tribe or Native Hawaiian organization may be determined to be eligible for inclusion on the National Register."

The National Register of Historic Places *Guidelines for Evaluating and Documenting Traditional Cultural Properties* defines a traditional cultural property as "one that is eligible for inclusion in the National Register because of its association with cultural practices or beliefs of a living community that (a) are rooted in that community's history, and (b) are important in maintaining the continuing cultural identity of the community" (Parker and King 1998). Practitioners in the United States, then, have categories similar to those identified in the *Burra Charter* as tools with which to develop a values-based approach to specific places with clearly defined boundaries.

Canada's recognized heritage values are also largely the same as those identified in the *Burra Charter*. The Heritage Branch of British Columbia's Ministry of Forests, Lands and Natural Resource Operations offers "Guidelines for Implementing Context Studies and Values-Based Management of Historic Places" (available from: http://www.for.gov.bc.ca/ftp/heritage/external/!publish/Web/Guidelines_for_Implementing_Context_Studies.pdf). They consider best practice on the local level to be a values-based approach that allows community identification and evaluation of historic places. The guidelines recommend, at minimum, a one-day workshop within a community to identify values and map historic places, covering the first two steps in a three-step planning process by developing a context study. The planning process is generalized in these steps:

1. a broad group of community members identify heritage values through systematically exploring their history, using a thematic framework;

2. the community identifies historic places that embody the identified values; and

3. informed by the context study developed in the first two steps, the community plans land use so that heritage values are preserved while development occurs.

The workshop is intended to delve into the community's history to identify the significant qualities that have made the community what it is today. The guidelines recommend using the five major themes of Parks Canada's thematic framework (http://www.pc.gc.ca/docs/r/system-reseau/sec2/sites-lieux17. aspx) to guide discussion and discovery around the community's history. These five themes are:

- Peopling the Land
- Developing Economies
- Governing Canada
- Building Social and Community Life
- Expressing Intellectual and Cultural Life

The guidelines outline five discussion questions to use with each theme, which are:

- Why did, and do, people live here?
- How and why is the community's historic and current economic development important to its heritage?
- How and why is the community's historic and current role as an administrative center significant?
- What is, and has been, special about the social and community life here?
- What is unique about the community's expressions of intellectual and cultural life over time?

The results of the workshop are then written into a report that informs planning at the local government level.

While the workshop guidance acknowledges that heritage values are classified in the categories of *historic, aesthetic, spiritual, social, cultural, and sci-*

entific, these questions alone will not necessarily elicit a full range of heritage values. Unless the community is prompted to consider scientific value, for example, these questions are not likely to elicit responses that question how we might know about or learn about the past.

How does Parks Canada's thematic framework compare to that used in the United States by the National Park Service (NPS)? The NPS's thematic framework is outlined in the booklet "History in the National Park Service: Themes & Concepts" (http://www.nps.gov/history/history/hisnps/NPSThinking/themes_concepts.htm), which includes eight themes, each with topics to help define them:

1. Peopling Places

2. Creating Social Institutions and Movements

3. Expressing Cultural Values

4. Shaping the Political Landscape

5. Developing the American Economy

6. Expanding Science and Technology

7. Transforming the Environment

8. Changing Role of the United States in the World Community

The similarities between these two frameworks are obvious (Australia and New Zealand also take a similar approach to their frameworks). In sum, for identifying basic and comparable values associated with cultural heritage, practitioners in the United States have the requisite tools to explore and embrace a values-based approach to identifying and honoring heritage values from diverse stakeholders for specific bounded places. These tools are based in existing laws, regulations, and practice, and while they use different words and approaches than those in the *Burra Charter*, there are no obvious barriers to taking a values-based approach, and there is no need to wait for a change in law or regulation.

Chapter 7

A Civic Engagement Ladder and Pyramid

Expectations for Civic Engagement

What is a reasonable expectation for civic engagement in a project or program? Stakeholders have different levels of commitment and their involvement will probably change over time depending on a wide variety of factors.
Social media theorist Clay Shirky (2003) observes that power law distribu-
tions such as the Pareto Principle arise in any social system where many
people express preferences among many options, including decisions about
participation. The often-cited Pareto Principle, or 80-20 rule, states that 20
percent of a group will produce 80 percent of the activity. Another such principle provides us an expectation about how we might expect an online community to "engage." In the world of online interaction, the 90-9-1 rule is often
cited, suggesting that 1 percent of participants create the content, 9 percent
reply, and 90 percent observe. While not always correct it is a useful reminder
that group participation is often unequal and unbalanced and a small percentage of contributors usually do a large percentage of the contributing. Such low
participation is not a phenomenon unique to the digital world. Saul Alinsky
(1945) cautioned activists against expecting extensive participation. He noted
that even in deeply rooted peoples' organizations, participation only ranged
between 5 and 7 percent.

One of the outcomes of effective civic engagement is broader and more
inclusive participation in any particular activity. It has the potential to have
a transformative effect, depending on both the participants and their level

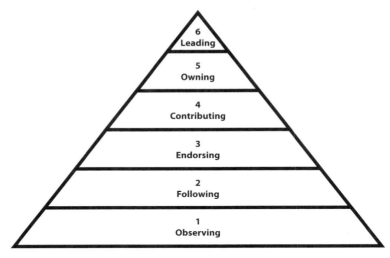

Figure 7.1   Engagement Pyramid (after Rosenblatt 2010).

of participation. Planning and enabling increased levels of participation can drive such change; therefore, it is useful to have an understanding of how people might move from being mildly interested observers to being fully engaged participants. Agents of social change must have the communications skills to develop a "call to action" that will help people achieve higher levels of engagement in their mission (Rosenblatt 2010).

The engagement pyramid (figure 7.1) can help to guide strategy in a way that is similar to community organizing. The vertical dimension of the pyramid represents increasing intensity of engagement from bottom to top as people move up a ladder of engagement. The horizontal dimension represents the number of people involved, reflecting power law principles. Combine the two and you get a pyramid with lots of mildly engaged people at the base and a small number of deeply engaged people at the top. Outside of the pyramid are a large number of people who are unaware or are aware but disinterested.

People tend to start at the bottom of the pyramid, and as they become more involved they climb the pyramid. Since there is no required end point and given the shrinking numbers at the top of the pyramid, it is to be expected that most people do not climb very high up the ladder of engagement for any specific project or cause.

With the advent of the digital information age and the development of digital habitats for online communities, it is increasingly common for communications and relationships at the bottom of the pyramid to be technology-based and more automated. People with easy access to websites, email, and social networking tend to be comfortable using those media to both prompt engagement and to become engaged. In contrast, at the top of the pyramid, relationships tend to be more personal and labor-intensive. In climbing the engagement ladder, personal relationships tend to become more critical for creating successful engagement. Websites and social media networking still play an important role in routine communications; however, there is no substitute for the human interaction. The engagement pyramid provides an overview that spans engagement in the electronic and the personal world (Rosenblatt 2010).

This model can help an organizer manage expectations and gauge levels of commitment and impact. For example, it is critical to consider how much time, money, and social capital people have available and to ensure that there are opportunities for a full range of levels of interest. The climb up the engagement pyramid often, but not always, starts at the very bottom. People become aware of something and then they assess whether they want to participate in some way. Becoming engaged in the group's activities with the goal of making effective change will eventually mean a commitment of time, money, and/or social capital. People will spend varying amounts of time at different stages. Sometimes it may be a brief stay, and other times it can be a longer commitment before moving to the next stage, or even dropping out.

We are interested in how such expectations about commitment might play out on the ground, so we will now examine the correlation between an engagement model and community participation over a period of time in the New Philadelphia archaeology project in Illinois.

The Engagement Pyramid in an Archaeological Project

In 2002, a collaborative project in Illinois that included universities, a state museum, and the local and descendant communities developed with the goal of locating and commemorating the earliest known town founded and platted by a freed African American. That town, New Philadelphia, was established in 1836 by Frank McWorter. It stood about twenty-five miles east of the Mississippi River, and it developed as a small, multiracial, rural community. By the beginning of the American Civil War, about 160 people resided in the town. In 1869, a railroad line that could have run through the town was instead routed about a mile north. Because of competition and the lack of commerce, the town soon began a slow decline. Residents moved to larger communities, like St. Louis and Chicago. By the 1920s, about six households remained in the town proper. Today, fallow fields, a few foundations, and a nationally significant archaeological site exist where the town once stood (Fennell 2010; Fennell et al. 2010; Shackel 2011).

When the New Philadelphia Association (NPA) in 2002 invited researchers to explore the heritage of New Philadelphia to help promote the mission of the organization, the institutions involved included the University of Maryland, the Illinois State Museum, and the University of Illinois. This effort developed into an important collaborative archaeology project that continually engaged the local and descendant communities.

When the research project began, the archaeologists involved moved rapidly up the engagement pyramid and became contributors, committing themselves to the overall goal of commemorating New Philadelphia. Archaeologists attended meetings with the community organizations and adopted their mission. Working with the community to develop an archaeological survey meant dedicating time, expense, and social capital toward the goal of preserving and interpreting the site to a larger audience. In 2002 and 2003, a team of volunteers performed a walkover survey of a fallow field and found thousands of artifacts related to the occupation of the town (Gwaltney 2004). In 2004, the University of Maryland was awarded a three-year National Science Foundation-Research Experiences for Undergraduates (NSF-REU) grant. This grant was awarded again in 2008 to the University of Illinois (Fennell et al. 2010).

The goal of the New Philadelphia project was to work collaboratively with the community to develop a more diverse story of the region's past (figure 7.2). The project's goal was to also provide the local community and descendant communities with enough historical and archaeological information to take ownership of a new meaning of the town's historic past and to enable them to preserve the place for the present and the future. This teaching and learning situation became an extraordinary experience in civic engagement and social justice in several ways (Shackel 2005).

Early in the project it became clear that the different stakeholders had very different views about the history of New Philadelphia. The majority of the local community consisted of observers. They came to the site to visit and to view the archaeological process. Newspaper articles ran in the local newspapers and community members became aware of the project. After a news re-

Figure 7.2 New Philadelphia archaeology students providing a tour of the townsite of New Philadelphia to descendants of the original settlers of the town. (Photograph by Paul A. Shackel.)

lease, which often made the front page in this small, rural community, archaeologists would walk into the local grocery store and people would recognize them and comment on the project. More difficult to detect was the number of people who followed the progress of the project on the Internet.

Racial tensions in the community were visible at the beginning of the archaeological survey. While the majority in the community were observers they did not necessarily endorse this heritage project; during the archaeological survey some local farmers drove by the field in their trucks and yelled that the archaeologists should leave town and go back to Chicago. Apparently, some community members felt threatened that the archaeologists were developing a heritage project that might not include or foreground their ancestors or their views of the past. Instead, it appeared that the focus was on the African American community, a group that no longer had descendants present in the surrounding areas (Shackel 2011). It became clear that it was important to think of ways to increase the number of people endorsing the project in a way that included both descendants and the local community.

The challenge for the archeology research team was to find a way to inspire observers to at least endorse, and perhaps even contribute to the project.

Figure 7.3   The website for the Center for Heritage Resource Studies at New Phila-delphia: http://www.heritage.umd.edu/chrsweb/new%20philadelphia/newphiladel-phia.htm.

Therefore, the complete sharing of knowledge in research, practice, and teach-ing became an important vehicle in trying to bridge these different groups with the intent to democratize the project. The research team posted all of their work on the Internet, including the archaeology, geophysics, deed, cen-sus, newspaper, and tax records, as well as the oral histories as soon as results became available (figure 7.3).

Transparency allows others to see how researchers make conclusions from data, and it also allows people to challenge those interpretations. It took some time for the New Philadelphia project to build up trust with the com-munity. However, this type of sharing demonstrated to the descendant and local communities that the research team was not sweeping into a community, taking data, and waiting to publish it at some future date. Rather, the team was sharing research questions and interpretive findings as they developed. This process allowed the New Philadelphia research team a chance to explain and support their interpretations, particularly those that directly challenged fam-ily histories and the public memory of the place (Shackel 2011). Sharing the broad array of data also allowed for observers to connect to the project when they recognized their ancestors' roles in the community. Some became followers and a few others became endorsers of the project.

When archaeologists began working on the project, New Philadelphia was known as an all-black town. However, the state and federal census data showed a very different picture. Throughout the town's entire history only about 25 to 35 percent of the town's population was classified by the census takers as black or mulatto. Some of the community's African American descendants were shocked because family oral traditions conveyed to them that their ancestors helped to develop an all-black town. Several in the white community were also surprised to learn that their relatives once lived in the same town and in close proximity to African Americans. Posting the census data and making it public to a wider audience helped to ease any friction that developed by challenging the traditional memory of the place. One of the beneficial outcomes of publicizing this history was that it allowed more families to claim ownership of New Philadelphia's past. Some of the members of the white community who were observers and followers slowly began to support and endorse the New Philadelphia archaeology project. More of them began to visit the site, and they also contributed to the oral history project. They came to a weekly lecture series that highlighted issues related to preservation, archaeology, race, and the Illinois frontier. Some even contributed to the lecture series, sharing with students and community members their memories and their relatives' memories of growing up in New Philadelphia (Shackel 2009).

Throughout the entire project the posting of data on the project's websites continued to be a valuable engagement tool. It allowed the research team to make available any new findings in a timely manner. Critiques and challenges continued throughout the entire project, and this feedback allowed the research team to understand how different stakeholders viewed and interpreted the past. Not only did the research team help to change the community's view of its past, the descendant community also influenced the way archaeologists viewed the community's past. For example, the project's initial research design included questions related to locating the town and understanding consumerism and diet on the Illinois frontier. After several meetings with some of the stakeholders, it became clear that some of the descendants of the original settlers, Frank and Lucy McWorter, wanted different elements of the past to be interpreted (Shackel 2011). Taking a leadership role, they worked to make the ideal of freedom part of the official meaning of New Philadelphia. They highlighted the fact that members of the McWorter family were involved in the Underground Railroad, and therefore, this meaning should be part of how New Philadelphia was remembered. The archaeology team followed their lead and embraced the idea of freedom as an important universal value that could be associated with the site and they worked with family members to link this value to New Philadelphia. The theme of freedom became important when nominating the townsite for listing in the National Register of Historic Places in 2005 and when it was designated as a National Historic Landmark (NHL) in 2009 (Shackel 2010).

While the NSF-REU fieldschool taught students how to excavate and identify and catalogue artifacts, the archaeology team also engaged students, community members, and descendants in a conversation about historic and contemporary issues related to race and racism. In the first half of the nineteenth century, Illinois had some of the most severely racist legislation among the northern states before the Civil War. Illinois passed Black codes in 1819, 1829, and 1853 which made it difficult for African Americans to attain full citizenship (Davis 1998, 165, 413; Simeone 2000, 157). Newspaper accounts and oral histories provide details of Ku Klux Klan (KKK) disturbances in the area from the post-World War I era through the 1960s. Several community elders recall seeing a Klan ride and cross burning close to New Philadelphia intended to chase away black workers who were part of a road crew constructing a local highway. Another community elder told a story of witnessing a KKK ride past her house one night when the Klan was seen in the vicinity of the home of a black man who lived close to the Illinois River. According to the story, the man went missing the next day. An African American descendant and member of the New Philadelphia Association is well versed in the accounts of the racism that his family endured while living in the town. Surrounding communities became sundown towns, meaning African Americans were not allowed in those communities after sunset (Loewen 2005; Shackel 2005). Recent federal census data indicates that only a few African American families currently claim Pike County as their home, and no African Americans live in the county to its immediate south. These stories and detailed project information is available online by choosing "New Philadelphia" at http://www.heritage.umd.edu.

Some local community members attended an open forum with the field school students to discuss issues of race and racism after viewing the series *Race—The Power of an Illusion* on public television. The film series dismantles myths associated with the construction of race, putting race and racism into historical context. In a group conversation, one white student spoke about how the film challenged her misconceptions about biological differences between blacks and whites. In another discussion, an African American student spoke about being profiled and harassed by St. Louis City police on several occasions. These comments and reactions to them led to a productive dialogue that allowed participants to imagine similar stereotyping and physical assaults that the early residents of New Philadelphia may have experienced. Community members also expressed their amazement about the history of the construction of race and endorsed the development of a multiracial past and present (Shackel 2007).

During one session several students asked how they could change racist attitudes in the United States. One student argued that racism could only change if individuals worked through it on a case-by-case basis; in other words, change the world one person at a time. Another student responded that we needed more legislation to create more anti-discrimination laws and help even the playing field. The conversations continued with these students fully engaged in the issue, owning it as something in which their own actions mattered (Shackel 2007).

Community members have made a commitment to developing an understanding of a multicultural past in New Philadelphia in order to help promote a multicultural present. It is important that power is redistributed in order to allow for real world multivocality; access and inclusion are part of this social responsibility. The NPA has affirmed that all of the stakeholders will be invited to participate in the association's mission to preserve the story of the site. The organization now has members of the McWorter family and other African American descendants on its governing board. Thus, in many ways, the engagement process has allowed the leadership to expand and be more inclusive.

The development of heritage is crucial to the survival of displaced communities (Oliver-Smith 2006). Uprooted communities, like New Philadelphia, draw upon their heritage to create their community. Bridging social capital, which crosses geography, ethnic groups, class, and age, brings people together from different communities to find common ground. In the case of New Philadelphia, new links created new concepts of community and boundaries that traditionally separated communities became blurred.

The archaeology team took a leadership role in nominating New Philadelphia for the National Register of Historic Places in 2005 and in constructing an effective argument for its designation as a National Historic Landmark four years later. Staff members and students worked diligently to achieve official federal recognition for the site and in developing a classroom lesson plan teachers could use in schools (King 2007). However, while experts worked hard to write these nominations, the documentation needed to be endorsed by the community and by politicians. Members of the descendant and local communities traveled to Washington, DC, to testify on behalf of New Philadelphia's status as a nationally significant site. Receiving the endorsement of politicians, including state senators and representatives and the governor, was important for placing New Philadelphia on the National Register of Historic Places. A few years later, then-Senator Barack Obama provided an endorsement for the NHL designation. Local and descendant community members also used their own networks to gain support from politicians to help achieve these designations.

Complicating the Model of Engagement

The New Philadelphia project is about using archaeology to help create a bridging social capital between archaeologists, the local community, and the many descendant groups. Linking descendant and local communities can lead to a more inclusive narrative and provide a broader understanding of past and present social and economic inequities. It can also bring various constituencies together to use the past to illuminate important social, political, and economic issues that we face today.

The archaeology project was developed with the endorsement of the New Philadelphia Association (NPA) for the purpose of preserving the townsite of New Philadelphia and commemorating its founder, Frank McWorter. The NPA took a leadership role in the preservation of this historic town and eventually invited the academic institutions to do archaeology in the community. The descendant community then began contributing to the preservation of the archaeology site. They took ownership of the interpretive message of the place, and now they are leading in the preservation of the town's history and land. The archaeologists involved in the project immediately endorsed the project and began to contribute to helping commemorate the townsite.

The case study of New Philadelphia shows some of the complexities of the engagement pyramid model. While the pyramid may provide the perception that there is a natural progression up the pyramid, the engagement process also needs to be thought of as nonlinear. In the case of New Philadelphia, there is an important blend of owning and observing. The NPA Board of Directors worked to become much more diverse, which has been critical to the ongoing success of the project. The board has included research team members as well as members of the local and descendant communities. A deep sense of volunteerism developed among these members. Those who took on the task of becoming board members of the New Philadelphia Association feel ownership of the project and continue to work hard to make it a success.

Archaeologists spent time working with various community organizations and spoke to groups, like the Lions Club, with the goal of making people more aware of the significance of the preservation effort and the meaning of the place. The archaeologists also became fully invested in the project and shared in the ownership as they sought and were awarded two National Science Foundation grants, which was a significant investment in resources and social capital in the mission and success of the project.

Some descendants began as observers, others were initially involved as endorsers, and others as contributors. Eventually some descendants took ownership of the preservation of the townsite as well as the interpretive message of the place. They took a leadership role in changing how the place is remembered and the landscape commemorated. This work has been an important contribution to creating a healthier community by bridging the various stakeholder groups to create an inclusive present, as well as a more inclusive past.

The engagement pyramid works as a conceptual tool, but it is not a rigid model. It becomes apparent that people do not necessarily climb the ladder, nor is it necessarily a natural phenomenon that all start as observers. Some may leap in at various engagement levels and they can move back down the ladder. Others may climb the ladder, although the length of spent at each station can vary considerably. People can endorse—as the politicians did for the New Philadelphia project—and then end their engagement. Other people start as leaders in a project, and coaxed others to endorse, contribute, and own. Some begin as contributors, but later become observers. Others may eventually sever all connections. People will judge for themselves the importance of their own involvement and respond accordingly.

Civic engagement has become a common phrase and common ambition. There are many models, much guidance, and an increasing amount of research into what works and how to improve engagement and collaboration. The engagement ladder and pyramid and the collaborative continuum are models that help us understand how to increase participation. We will now turn to civic engagement in the context of higher education and service learning.

Chapter 8

The (Re)Evolving Mission
of Higher Education

What Is the Role of the University?

In a 2009 essay in the *New York Times,* Harvard University president Drew
Gilpin Faust states that the American university is undergoing a crisis of purpose, as universities will increasingly be called upon to help solve many of
the social problems facing our nation. While many Americans may have the
notion that university education should serve the market, this market model
conflicts with the idea that "universities are meant to be producers not just of
knowledge but also of (often inconvenient) doubt" (Faust 2009). Faust recognizes that people need jobs; however, they also seek meaning, understanding,
and perspective. She writes, "The question should not be whether we can afford to believe in such purposes in these times, but whether we can afford
not to." Doubt, as it supports the ability to question our own individual ideas,
beliefs and values, as well as those of our society, is an essential ingredient for
transformational learning.

For several decades, critics of American higher education have recognized the crisis of purpose that Faust describes. Colleges and universities have
been called upon to renew their historic commitment to service. Government
and business leaders as well as social policy experts are asking universities to
assume a greater role in addressing society's increasing problems and meeting
growing human needs. New, developing programs in higher education are fo-

Archaeology, Heritage, and Civic Engagement, Barbara J. Little and Paul A. Shackel, p. 95–110.

cusing on building and sustaining relationships with neighbors and communities. The Association of American Colleges and Universities (2010) suggests that recent educational innovations that advance civic engagement, such as thematically linked learning communities, community-based research, collaborative projects, service learning, mentored internships, reflective experiential learning, and study abroad, are all helping students advance toward this essential learning goal. While there is a call for colleges and universities to be active in local and national communities, the experiences of each institution vary considerably.

The turn of the twenty-first century has some issues in common with those at the turn of the twentieth century. At that time, social capital was at a low point. A century ago, urban decay, unchecked industrialization, and massive immigration strained society. In the late 1880s, in response to these social problems, Smith College became involved in social welfare programs in New York City to help the urban poor. The college settlement movement grew and other colleges throughout the country became engaged in their local communities to address social problems. At the turn of the century, Americans believed that universities could lead the way in social reform (Berube and Berube 2010, 4-5).

By the end of World War II and through the Cold War era, the American university in general lost its mission of serving communities. Rather, attention turned toward the needs of outside interests that provided financial support. Significant research funding came from the military-industrial complex, and by the 1970s, an increasing amount of research in universities was sponsored by private industries. Jennifer Washburn (quoted in Berube and Berube 2010, 52–53) wrote in 1980 that, "the single greatest threat to the future of American higher education is the intrusion of a market ideology into the heart of academic life." In *The Moral Collapse of the University*, Bruce Wilshire (1990, xxiv) charged that higher education had lost its way, and he declared an imperative to restore the university's moral course and to think about what it means to be human.

While there have been some serious efforts to respond to such critiques, as we will note below, it appears that the line separating corporations and academia has been blurred in recent years. The *New York Times* (Bowley 2010, 1, 4) reported that presidents and other senior officials from top tier universities are increasingly serving on corporate boards. While it is prestigious to have a university official on the board, these academics offer different perspectives, and they often provide diversity to the corporate board. In a recent survey by the *Chronicle of Higher Education,* almost half (19) of the presidents from the top 40 research institutions with the largest operating budgets sat on at least one company board, and a few presidents belonged to several boards. The corporate model has increasingly infiltrated the university system and many public institutions are now required to bring in greater revenue through research and grants to fund the operations of the institution. A common critique arising from the changing economic structure is that traditionally public-supported institutions are now, at best, "public assisted," meaning that government no longer supports higher education (Bowley 2010, 1, 4).

In 1985, recognizing the problematic position of higher education, university presidents from Georgetown, Stanford, and Brown and the president of the Education Commission of the States took the initiative in developing nationwide awareness about the benefits of service and engagement. These institutions took the lead to develop Campus Compact as a resource to enhance civic engagement in U. S. higher education. This coalition consists of college and university presidents representing public and private, two- and four-year institutions. Over 1,100 institutions representing over 6 million students pledge to advance community service and support service learning initiatives to prepare students for civic responsibilities. Campus Compact "promotes public and community service that develops students' citizenship skills, helps campuses forge effective community partnerships, and provides resources and training for faculty seeking to integrate civic and community-based learning into the curriculum" (Campus Compact 2013 (a)). In 1996 Campus Compact members also agreed on a presidents' statement, of principles which: 1) endorses the importance of public service, 2) sanctions the importance of speaking out on issues of public concern, 3) supports productive collaborations between colleges and communities, 4) endorses citizenship-building service activities, and 5) supports service learning (Campus Compact 2013 (b); Jacoby 1996). These statements provide greater support to enhance students' abilities to participate in civil life and civil society.

In 1999, Campus Compact had an important role in drafting the "Presidents' Declaration on the Civic Responsibility of Higher Education," which has so far been signed by presidents from over 570 campuses. It is a challenge to "higher education to re-examine its public purposes and its commitments to the democratic ideal" (Campus Compact 2013 (c)). The Declaration" takes seriously the growing decline in social capital, stating that:

We also challenge higher education to become engaged, through actions and teaching, with its communities. We have a fundamental task to renew our role as agents of our democracy. This task is both urgent and long-term. There is growing evidence of disengagement of many Americans from the communal life of our society in general, and from the responsibilities of democracy in particular. We share a special concern about the disengagement of college students from democratic participation.

Civic Engagement and Service Learning

Colleges and universities—particularly land grant institutions—have a clear obligation to be engaged in communities, especially those with which they share common boundaries. In *Civic Responsibility and Higher Education,* Thomas Ehrlich (2000c, vi) writes that:

> Civic engagement means working to make a difference in the civic life of our communities and developing the combination of knowledge, skills, values and motivation to make that difference. It means promoting the quality of life in a community, through both political and non-political processes.

The model for engagement within communities works best when college students and communities can both benefit from collaboration.

If heritage work is to participate effectively in solving social problems, it is important that the heritage disciplines participate in reenergizing civic involvement. Along with our colleagues, we have argued that archaeology is an effective tool for civic engagement (Little and Shackel 2007), and the same is true for heritage work in general. Universities are notorious for guarding disciplinary boundaries, and yet, remain some of the most obvious and powerful incubators for work that cuts across disciplinary and generational boundaries.

Universities have a recognized obligation to address social needs (Bok 1982). Well-designed service learning experiences can promote civic responsibility and foster collaborative and problem-based learning (Ehrlich 2000a). Service learning in higher education can occur in many different ways. Ideally, it is not about volunteerism, where people with assets come into a community and provide resources and volunteer to help solve other people's problems (Kendall 1990). Instead, effective service learning is about doing things *with* others rather than *for* others. Therefore, it is important to create a dialogue with the community before planning any work and determining tasks. The needs of the community define the service tasks. The community must also have the opportunity to participate in the teaching and learning process. Projects should be mutually beneficial for the community and the university. Reciprocity allows students to develop a greater sense of belonging and responsibility as members of a larger community.

This distinction between volunteerism and collaboration is an important one and it takes intentional effort to achieve collaboration. In her essay "Educating for Citizenship," Caryn McTighe Musil (2003) proposes a framework to understand the phased relationship between levels of learning, the scope of connection between students and a community, and the benefits of such connections. Her categories are based on the kinds of service learning experiences provided to students in the United States, which means that most of the situations are those in which relatively privileged students are challenged to work with less privileged communities.

Six levels of civic scope correspond with phases of education, levels of knowledge, definition of community, and benefits (see table 8.1). In the lowest three levels, students are effectively disconnected and without knowledge of a historical perspective or any cultural vantage point that is not their own. The exclusionary phase could be considered analogous to the overly caricatured ivory tower, where scholars have no interest and no incentive to share their research or expertise with the uneducated public. Similarly, in the oblivious or naïve phases, there is little consideration of historical context or cultural differences. The bandwagon effect that applauds public outreach because it is the "thing to do," because it supposedly meets public involvement goals for compliance-driven projects can generate efforts to supply the public with accessible information that is of very little benefit except to the self-selected curious few.

In the "charitable" phase, the community is seen as in need of assistance and the civic scope is one of civic altruism. The level of knowledge is awareness of deprivations within a community and of multiculturalism, although the giver's culture is seen as the normal center. The benefits of civic altruism are the sufferer's immediate needs and the giver's feelings. In the case of student education, an example may be charitable work in a homeless shelter. In the case of heritage work, an example may be a scholar coming to the aid of the scientifically illiterate public by providing education about the best way to look at the past.

TABLE 8.1   EDUCATIONAL PHASES LEADING TO CIVIC ENGAGEMENT AND CIVIC PROSPERITY. (ADAPTED FROM MUSIL 2003:8 FOR LITTLE AND SHACKEL 2007).

Phase	Community is:	Civic Scope	Levels of Knowledge	Benefits
Exclusionary	only your own	civic disengagement	one vantage point (yours); monocultural	a few and only for a while
Oblivious	a resource to mine	civic detachment	observational skills; largely monocultural	one party
Naïve	a resource to engage	civic amnesia	no history; no vantage point; acultural	random people
Charitable	a resource that needs assistance	civic altruism	awareness of deprivations; affective kindliness and respect; multicultural but yours is still the norm center	the giver's feelings and the sufferer's immediate needs
Reciprocal	a resource to empower and be empowered by	civic engagement	legacies of inequality; values of partnering; intercultural competency; arts of democracy; multiple vantage points; multicultural	society as a whole in the present
Generative	an interdependent resource filled with possibilities	civic prosperity	struggles for democracy; interconnectedness; analysis of interlocking systems; intercultural competencies; arts of democracy; multiple interactive vantage points; multicultural	everyone now and in the future

Each of these four phases could fall into the category of volunteerism. Volunteering in the sense of service to others is a very important value. However, it is not necessarily conducive to service learning. It is not until the final two of Musil's phases that an engagement project qualifies as service learning done in partnership *with* community.

In the penultimate phase, which is "reciprocal," the community is a resource to empower and be empowered by. The benefits are seen as accruing to society as a whole in the present. This scope is that of civic engagement. The levels of knowledge are an awareness of the legacies of inequality, intercultural competency, multiculturalism and multiple vantage points, the values of partnering, and the arts of democracy. Examples of this type of project in archeology and broader heritage projects across the globe continue to grow.

What will move heritage work to the generative level, where the civic scope is that of civic prosperity and the benefits accrue in the present as well as in the future? We have suggested (Little and Shackel 2007) that it is a matter of critical mass and creating a disciplinary expectation. Movements require intention and persistence. Just as recognition of the legacies of inequality cannot exist without broad historical and cultural perspectives, successful struggles for true participatory democracy cannot occur without reciprocity and mutual empowerment. Civic prosperity cannot occur without civic engagement.

Service Learning and Critical Reflection

Service learning is about service and it is about learning, and both should be of equal weight in the student's experience. Service learning is a means for students to become better citizens, and it is a way to build upon existing community assets (Jacoby 1996, 5). Service learning must have some component of critical reflection, which is a key to learning. It also needs to integrate theory and practice, and it should address the issues underlying social problems. A program in service learning should help students strengthen their sense of social responsibility. It can enhance cognitive, personal, and spiritual development. Service learning should also heighten the student's understanding of human differences and commonality and sharpen their ability to solve problems creatively. The goal of any service learning experience is to help the student develop skills to work collaboratively (Jacoby 1996, xvii; see also Nassaney 2009).

In a successful service learning endeavor, the community will benefit by having new energy and additional university resources and assistance to support—and sometimes to expand—an existing mission or to develop new services, or both. Students coming into the project with different perspectives and university training can provide fresh approaches to solving problems. The community is also actively engaged in the teaching and learning process and can contribute in ways that complement what the faculty provides to students (Jacoby 1996, xvii).

In all service learning experiences, critical reflection is a very important component that can address spiritual and personal development, an appreciation of human diversity and commonalities, and problem solving. Recall Drew Gilpin Faust's emphasis on the importance of doubt. Doubt provides a path toward understanding and investigating important social issues, and it is also a venue for students to explore their own identity and see how the experience may have changed their thoughts and actions (McEwen 1996).

Educators have the task of developing an engaged scholarship that has a meaningful critical pedagogy. Students should be able to engage in debate and dialogue related to relevant social problems. They should not only be a part of civic life, but also make a difference in shaping it (Giroux 2007, 5). Critical reflection is an opportunity to place the learning experience into a larger context and show the complexity and varied histories that exist. The student should be able to enter into a critical dialogue rather than accept current social and political situations unquestioningly. They should be capable of questioning deep-seated assumptions and myths.

Critical reflection about the roots of some of the issues important to communities will help to stimulate discussions about how to make changes that address those issues. Reflection allows students to interrogate the status quo, question how society is organized, and how these structures reproduce social problems, inequalities, and injustices. Students need to first recognize the problem or issue, then step back and examine the factors that perpetuate these conditions. The next step is for the student to identify what needs to change to solve the problem. In some cases, transformational learning occurs. Students "struggle to solve a problem where our usual ways of doing or seeing do not work, and we are called to question the validity of what we think we know, or critically examine the very premise of our perceptions of the problem" (Eyler and Giles 1999, 133). Transformational learning does not happen often in a person's life, nor does one change one's perspective easily. The transformation occurs when we start to question such mundane, often unseen structures, as government budgetary priorities, zoning regulations, or access to education, medical attention, or employment—in other words, question the assumptions about the way society operates (Eyler and Giles 1999, 143).

This transformation may lead to actions taken to advance some interests over others or change arrangements that are already quite congenial to some people in the community. Some scholars question whether the ultimate goal for service learning should be social change, or at the very least, educating students who will be agents of social change (Lempert 1995). There has been some backlash against service learning from reactionary corners. There are an increasing number of lawsuits by people who feel that it is not legitimate to require service in a college or university setting. Some parents, administrators, boards, and alumni do not welcome the idea of students questioning fundamental arrangements of their society (Eyler and Giles 1999, 132). Henry Giroux (2007, 3–4) makes the case that critical thinking is under assault, especially in education. The strong development of radical reactionary ideology has shown a deep bias against appeals to reason, dialogue, and secular humanism. "Not only the American public but many educators have lost a meaningful language for linking schooling to democracy, convinced that education is now about job training, competitive market advantage, patriotic correctness, and a steady supply of labor for the national security state" (3).

In a service learning project, students are expected to learn and not just serve. Working collaboratively with people who have different experiences, expectations, and needs provides a ready environment for learning. Such opportunities exist not only for the students and community participants, but also for the credentialed researchers. Recognizing and attempting to meet the obligation of service from a university setting can lead to radical transformation of whole disciplines, as the experience of archaeology has discovered since the passage of NAGPRA in 1990. Collaboration changes the ways in which science and scholarship are carried out.

Impetus for collaboration often comes from outside of the mainstream, but it can be sustained by institutionalizing into the mainstream. An example of that is the National Science Foundation's requirement to consider broader societal impacts, established in the mid-1990s. The understanding of what engagement means has grown, and there is now a broader understanding that "community-based" is not the same thing as "community-engaged." Similarly, sharing the results of research or recruiting volunteers and students as "citizen scientists" to increase public science literacy is not the same as participatory action research where the public gets involved in the full spectrum of research, from forming research design to analysis to interpretation. It has been difficult for the science community to embrace the idea that community-engaged research can be as rigorous as work that is done in more traditionally distanced ways (Ramaley et al. 2009). Judith Ramaley and her co-authors (2009) have suggested that the case for research relevant to both researchers and communities can be framed simply as "Who cares about the questions? And who cares about the answers?"

Putting both questions and answers to good use is a goal for heritage work. Service learning projects are necessarily concerned with developing larger contexts, because it helps us understand where our work articulates with broader historical, social, economic, and political issues and democratic values. Understanding the larger context also allows us to reflect on our experience in the community and deepen our understanding of the world and the root causes of the need for service. In a service learning context, students can explore how they feel about their learning experiences and why, and how they relate to their civic values (Ehrlich 2000b). The student should be able to question the received narrative in society and enter into a critical dialogue rather than accepting that narrative unquestioningly. *They should see their work as participating in an unfinished democracy.*

If, for example, an archaeology project is exploring issues related to race, then students should also study the development and history of race and racism. The same should be true with explorations into questions about class and gender. Students need to reflect on how and why disparities exist in communities and societies, and how these differences may create differences in material culture and wealth. They can explore the history of contemporary policies that reinforce these disparities today.

Service Learning Examples in Archaeological Heritage

Nassaney (2009; also see Nassaney and Levine 2009) discusses the importance of developing academic programs that have connections to the wider community. For instance, Uzi Baram (2009, 110–121) examines race and class during his service learning program at the Rosemary Cemetery in Sarasota, Florida (figure 8.1). The cemetery was founded in the 1880s, and buried there are some of the founding families of the city. Working with community members to place the cemetery on the National Register of Historic Places, Baram's students recorded the grave markers and found African American burials in what was always believed to be a segregated city. For generations, people had assumed this segregation lasted beyond death. While this contradiction exists, this work was also placed within the larger context of the politics of race and class. While the Rosemary District became a traditionally poor and African American section of Sarasota, students were challenged to look at the surrounding gentrification and how it is displacing a community. The African American community had become marginalized and silenced in the memory of a place. The politics of gentrification became a powerful and eye-opening experience for many of the students.

In Winston-Salem, North Carolina, community leaders invited Paul Thacker (2009) and his undergraduate students to work with local residents during the redevelopment of a neighborhood known as Happy Hill (figure 8.2). This collaborative work focused on an early schoolhouse that served the

Figure 8.1   Rosemary Cemetery with development in the background. (Image courtesy of Uzi Baram.)

African American community and was guided by the following criteria: 1) collaboration between academic researchers and community members during problem formulation, 2) democratizing knowledge by validating multiple sources of knowledge and promoting the use of multiple methods of discovery and dissemination, and 3) a goal of social action for the purpose of achieving social change and social justice.

Happy Hill originally consisted of a set of slave cabins and a farmhouse. Because of a strong Moravian influence, the slaves were emancipated in the early nineteenth century, and the area became an enclave for African Americans. One of the important features the community wanted to locate was the African American schoolhouse. While the archaeology project did not locate the schoolhouse, community organizers and archaeologists view this project as an important program that helped to democratize the archaeology project and generated knowledge of the descendant community. The project revealed an important history that gave the community a deeper connection to the past and the surrounding land. The project placed significant symbolic value on these resources associated with the African American community, and it gave this community an important voice in subsequent development in the area.

Figure 8.2   Paul Thacker and a Wake Forest undergraduate student conducting a resistivity survey of the Happy Hill site. (Image Courtesy of Kenneth Robinson.)

The project also allowed students to work in the diverse surrounding community of Wake Forest, an experience that helped students to acknowledge white privilege (Thacker 2009, 161).

Connecting the archaeology to current social, political, or economic problems is important for making a service learning program in archaeology relevant, important, and necessary. For instance, immigration and migration are important parts of our national stories and national identity, and it can be important to connect these historic phenomena with contemporary debates about immigration. Immigrants founded the United States and moved great distances around the continent. More recently, some in the U.S. Congress are resurrecting many of the xenophobic fears that were part of the national debate from its early settlement through the twentieth century. The migration of people of different skin color, different languages, and different customs has led to the building of walls along the southern border of the United States. Some local and state laws have sanctioned English as the only official language, and other laws related to employment and housing have been passed. Issues surrounding historic migration can provide an excellent opportunity to address diversity and tolerance today. Having community members participate in learning opportunities and the teaching of these issues can be an important part of the discussions.

The Center for Heritage Resource Studies at the University of Maryland is providing an engaged learning experience for students in the neighborhoods surrounding the University of Maryland in Prince George's County. These communities developed during the late nineteenth century and then had significant growth in the post-World War II era as a suburb for Washington, DC. During the 1970s, white flight led to accelerated urban decay, and many communities' ethnic composition changed from predominantly white to African American. More recently, new Latino immigrants have made some of these communities their home.

The Lakeland community is an example of a service learning project underway at the University of Maryland. Lakeland is an African American enclave adjacent to the University of Maryland and in the City of College Park (figure 8.3). The community developed as a racially segregated suburb in the 1890s with whites living on the west side of the railroad tracks and blacks living on the east side. By the beginning of the twentieth century, the entire community was inhabited by African Americans. Many of the residents worked at the University in various service jobs. Nearly the entire community stood within the 100-year flooding zone. By the early 1960s, a large number of houses did not meet modern housing standards. The City of College Park requested federal support for a flood control project and funding for redevelopment and home renovations. The end product was the displacement of about two-thirds of the community. One-third of the community was replaced by a mix of subsidized housing and high-density apartments that are now occupied by University of Maryland students. The other one-third of the community, the portion on the eastern side of the railroad, was mined for sand and gravel during the 1976 construction of a line for the Washington-area rapid transit system. The federal government compensated the larger community by developing this area into a natural recreation area, which is now called Lake Artemisia (Lakeland 2013).

In the fall of 2008, members of the Lakeland Community Heritage Project came to the Center for Heritage Resource Studies and asked for assistance to help them rediscover their community's heritage. Several of the board members of the project wanted to know more about the history of their community, and they took great pride in the history of education in Lakeland. Several meetings were held during the semester to develop a research plan for moving forward. Undergraduate and graduate students worked with community members in doing research, collecting photographs, and performing oral histories.

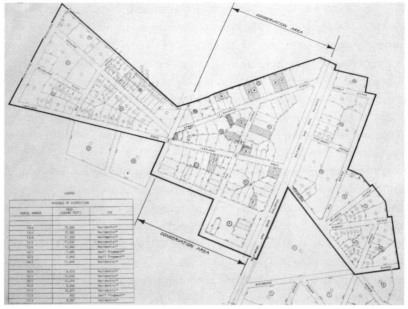

Figure 8.3   Lakeland Disposition Map dating to the 1960s, prior to the demolition of the eastern and western portions of the community. The area noted as the conservation zone remains today; the western portion is apartments; and the eastern portion has been submerged and is known as Lake Artemisia. (Photograph by Paul A. Shackel.)

Students doing research and interacting with community members revealed a unique and interesting history related to Lakeland's development of an educational system in a society that promoted segregation. The development of schools was community driven and Lakeland opened its first school in 1903. In 1917, a larger structure replaced the original school. Then in 1925 and 1928, they received funds from the Julius Rosenwald Fund to establish an elementary school and a high school, respectively. From 1928 until 1950, the Lakeland High School served as a regional educational, cultural, and social center for the African American community. Being the only African American high school in the area, people came from many parts of the county to attend school. The only other option would be to attend school in Washington, DC. Many of the oral histories of community members were performed by University of Maryland students. These led to an understanding of how the Lakeland school served many important functions, especially helping to create a social network among the different African American communities in the area, bridging social capital (Lakeland 2013).

Lakeland Heritage Days have become a yearly celebration of the community's past, and other events driven by community members have helped to bring together many members of the Lakeland community, near and far, to celebrate their past connections and plan for a renewed and viable community. The community heritage project now has a web page (Lakeland 2013), and their community history has been published (Lakeland Community Heritage Project 2009). University of Maryland classes in historic preservation have been held in Lakeland, uncovering more information about the community's origins. Additionally, two former graduate students served as board members for the Lakeland Community Heritage Project.

Students continue to work with community members to examine the history of housing, and they reflect on how housing has changed in our lifetime. Racism, immigration, redlining, and white flight are all important issues that led to the browning and graying of American cities and older suburbs, and the increased poverty in these areas is a product of the attack on the government programs that serve their populations. Schools continue to decay, crime is a problem, and Medicaid and Medicare programs continue to be cut. A program that makes these issues relevant to the student allows them to reflect on how these conditions developed. It is both political and powerful. In this context, service learning can be seen as a response to government downsizing and increasing privatization in a decreasingly regulated world.

Institutionalizing Service Learning

How does such work become institutionalized within higher education? One way is the embedding of requirements set by funding organizations, such as that previously mentioned at the National Science Foundation. Another is to ensure that service learning becomes part of the normal requirements of academic disciplines. Within Campus Compact, the mission and purpose of The Research University Civic Engagement Network (TRUCEN) is to advance civic engagement and engaged scholarship among research universities. The Network has adopted three goals to advance this mission (Campus Compact (d)):

1. Encourage community-engaged scholarship by identifying its dimensions and demonstrating how it satisfies criteria for rigorous scholarship established by and expected from research universi-

ties. There are core dimensions within this goal: The *purpose* of the research must be to benefit society, broadly defined, as opposed to developing new knowledge solely for its own sake....The *process* must be collaborative....The *impact* of engaged research must benefit society and extend beyond making a difference only within an academic field.

2. Encourage research on different forms of civic engagement and give greater visibility to this growing field of scholarship.

3. Encourage greater commitment to curricular and co-curricular activities that promote students' civic understanding and engagement, and scholarly efforts to understand and articulate the outcomes, challenges, and best practices for doing so.

As institutions of higher learning are being called upon to address the many needs of society, significant civic engagement programs are increasingly recognized as imperative. Civically-engaged service learning can help foster students' appreciation of human differences and it can help teach individuals to live peacefully and productively in communities that value persons of different races, genders, physical and mental abilities, religions, class backgrounds, and sexual orientations. As heritage workers, we need to think about critically analyzing and exposing the many "isms" that existed in the past and survive in the present. If we want to counter structural violence and cultural violence, then we need to dismantle the structures of oppression where we can. We are well positioned to research the relationships between past and present and their interdependence. We need to recognize categories of identity and social relationships and aim to historicize them when working with communities on their heritage issues. We also need to explore diversity in the past and promote tolerance and peaceful relationships in the present.

No story is complete if it is told from just one perspective. Scholars in positions of privilege within universities can commit to participate in meaningful ways in raising consciousness, working through the issues required for public judgment, and collaboratively crafting resolutions to critical issues. Heritage workers can help to create a past that recognizes and explicitly learns from hidden injustices and difficult histories.

Chapter 9

What Is at Stake?

Unsilencing the Violence of Labor Heritage

The coal patch town of Lattimer in northeastern Pennsylvania is the site of one of the most horrific events in American labor history. On September 10, 1897, twenty-five miners were shot dead on a public road by a sheriff and his posse, and many more were wounded as Slavic immigrants protested for better pay and better working conditions (figure 9.1). The event has been mostly forgotten in American history (Shackel and Roller 2012).

When the *Wall Street Journal* reviewed the book *The Guns of Lattimer* in 1978, a historical fiction account of the events leading up to the event, the reviewer wrote, "It is tempting to ask Mr. Novak why we really need the book. The incident occurred more than 80 years ago. It sounds like a unique event that would best be forgotten. Besides, American society has changed; American bosses don't act that way toward blue-collar workers anymore" (Wysocki 1978:24).

Since the 1980s, the right of collective bargaining has been under attack in the United States. In 2012 alone, Republican-controlled legislatures in three midwestern states have challenged and weakened union representation. An increasing number of people are now bound to make lower wages and have fewer benefits. We believe that heritage is increasingly relevant to working-class people, nationally and globally.

Heritage work can help illuminate the roots of contemporary social, economic, and political injustices. Better understanding of historical conditions allows us to explain how many of these social inequities developed, and to

Figure 9.1   Remembrance Rock is located near the Lattimer massacre site. While the community tried for many decades to place a memorial at the site, it was not until 1972 that this stone was erected. (Image courtesy of Kristin Sullivan.)

show how they operate in the contemporary world and might be dismantled. Examining the material conditions of life for traditionally marginalized groups, such as the poor, women, and undocumented workers, allows our heritage practices to be visible, relevant, and potentially transformational.

Shackel (2013) ties incidents of injustice against mineworkers across time and space from the nineteenth-century northeastern United States to twenty-first-century South Africa, emphasizing that the same type of labor injustice continues. Labor laws were weak in the United States in the nineteenth century, allowing significant injury and death due to the lack of safety regulations. Although laws have been strengthened in response to collective action by labor unions, these conditions, in a sense, have been exported to other coun-tries, only to have the same results. Such continuity contrasts sharply with the opinion of the *Wall Street Journal* reviewer of *The Guns of Lattimer.*

The 1897 Lattimer massacre was the result of a conflict between immigrant laborers and coal operators in the anthracite region of northeastern Pennsylva-nia. Living in poverty in scattered shanty towns, with inadequate housing, no sanitation infrastructure, and none of the comforts normally found among the native-born or naturalized working class, the miners struck for equal pay and better living conditions. A conflict with the sheriff and his posse left twenty-five immigrant men of East European descent dead and nearly forgotten. The majority died of wounds from being shot in the back as they fled the scene. Not surprisingly, the event is missing from the official memory of our country, and it reflects the control that the wealthy elite have over the memory of the industri-alization of America (Beik 2002; Novak 1978; Shackel and Roller 2012).

Although the massacre has all but been erased from national memory, local community historians, clergy, community leaders, families, and a hand-ful of academics have kept the story alive. In 2009, the anthropology program at the University of Maryland committed itself to helping to raise the profile of the event with the goal of making it part of the national public memory. In 2010, an archaeological survey was undertaken in the area with the collabora-tion of BRAVO (Battlefield Restoration & Archaeological Volunteer Organi-zation). The survey located the massacre site, finding bullets and shell casings dating to the era of the massacre. This provided concrete evidence of the event, which was highly contested for over a century. The sheriff and his posse shot into the line of strikers at about the same place where oral histories suggest the initial confrontation occurred. Although some of the posse argued at the court trial that the miners began the altercation, it is now clear that the miners were fired upon (Shackel and Roller 2012; Shackel et al. 2011).

A similar event occurred recently in South Africa where mine workers struck at Lonmin's Marikana platinum mine. The strike began on August 10, 2012, when 3,000 mine workers walked off the job because they were con-cerned about living conditions, wage inequality, and poverty. Frustrated from a lack of economic progress, the workers initially rejected the long-term lead-ership of the National Union Mineworkers (NUM) for the militant Associa-tion of Mineworkers and Construction Union (AMCU). The beginning of the strike led to ten deaths, including miners, police officers, and mine security staff (De Wet 2012; Laing 2012; Tabane 2012).

On August 16, 2012, the police could not control the crowd with tear gas, water cannons, and barbed wire. The police fired live rounds into the crowd of miners for three minutes. Reports indicate that this was the deadliest force used in South Africa since the end of apartheid in 1994. The police killed 34 strikers, and a postmortem examination of the dead indicates that the majority of the strikers were shot in the back while fleeing the confrontation. The autopsy report contradicts the police account that they fired on an attacking mob. Those miners who were captured and imprisoned later filed over 150 complaints that they were tortured while in police custody (De Wet 2012; Laing 2012; Tabane 2012). By the end of September 2012, the company and the workers solved their wage dispute. With the help of the South African Council of Churches along with the moderate union, and the exclusion of the AMCU, a minimum entry wage was set and is to be enacted within two years (De Wet 2012).

One of the most powerful tools heritage workers have to confront inequalities today is the example of the past, which can be used to illuminate connections to current social, political, and economic issues. Many of the social injustices that existed in the United States over a hundred years ago still exist and have been exported to other parts of the world. Most large-scale corporations work to make labor inequity invisible, keeping workers and their concerns at the periphery of any discussion related to issues of social justice in the workplace. By bringing to light the conditions of the past and connecting these issues to the present, we can make some of these difficult histories a platform from which to discuss the continued prevalence of these inequities. If you can change the memory of an event, you change what is important in the public memory, and you change the conversation as people work through the lessons they draw from the past.

The Lattimer massacre is not part of the national public memory, and the event at Lonmin's Marikana platinum mine has been quickly forgotten, at least by the mainstream English-speaking media. As corporations and labor struggle for control over the public memory of any event, forgetting becomes an effective strategy to subvert the memory of marginalized groups.

Discussing the political endpoint of heritage, Magnus Nilsson (2011) distinguishes between identity-based heritage and the heritage of labor. Drawing on the work of literary theorist Walter Benn Michaels, Nilsson proposes that what those embracing identities based on racial, ethnic, gendered or other differences want is recognition and respect, and for their difference to be treated as equal and not inferior. In contrast, what the working class wants is to cease being, not to need to be recognized as different. Because of class politics, heritage may become counterproductive to the struggle unless it contributes to the struggle for economic justice. The editors of *Heritage, Labour and the Working Classes* (Smith et al. 2011, 13) summarize one of the lessons they draw from the contributions to that volume:

> the heritage of working class people is not only often advanced in the context of attempts to forget it or obscure its political and cultural significance, working class heritage, whatever its form, is also intrinsically linked to projects of protest and social justice. Remembering working class heritage, and understanding its links to social justice agendas, is given moral urgency in the face of ongoing attempts to forget and suppress labour history. Meanwhile, the moral imperative is given further imperatives as discourses of social justice in the U.S. are ridiculed and international debates about immigration and class become increasingly reactionary in the context of the current global economic crisis.

With the heritage of labor, then, the challenge is to redefine the way people remember and think about class, conflict, human rights, and representation. How do we make events like those that occurred at Lattimer and Lonmin's Marikana mine part of public memory? And, if we make such sites of labor and struggle known on a global scale, can we heighten attention to similar events and avoid the bloodshed that occurred in South Africa?

Michel-Rolph Trouillot (1995, 15) notes that a dominant narrative often means that there is a process of selective remembering that leaves some accounts out of the story. The history that is not silenced is what the general narrative of the past becomes. Not all sources have the same value throughout a community, and to some extent the dominant narrative often has components of a fictitious story. Trouillot (1995) cautions us to be aware of the silenced past. We envision that the heritage fields can unsilence the violence of both the past and the present.

A Heritage of Complicity

When considering the past and its legacy and repercussions today, consider the words of Desmond Tutu (1999, 31) concerning apartheid in South Africa: "the past, far from disappearing or lying down and being quiet, is embarrassingly persistent, and will return and haunt us unless it has been dealt with adequately. Unless we look the beast in the eye we will find that it returns to hold us hostage." It is important to make explicit in our public and academic interpretations that enslavement is very much a part of the history of labor, and that it still exists today. Such connections can become part of a dialogue in any civically engaged project that calls for social justice.

When we discuss issues of labor at historic sites, we are often faced with stories that glorify the importance of the development of capitalism, and often we learn very little about the injustices that workers faced. While many of the histories of nineteenth-century northeastern U.S. industry celebrate the advances of the industrial revolution, managers in Lowell, Massachusetts were known for sexually abusing the women who worked at the spinning machines in the factories. This story is not part of the official memory of industry. David Williams (2005, 42) describes it as a kind of sex slavery, a practice that was common in the factory system. Women who worked in the factories were tainted for life, as people assumed that managers abused them. Many former factory workers never married and were frequently called "spinsters."

Americans most often associate enslavement in the United States with the plantation system, specifically in the southern states. Researchers have written a significant amount about plantation slavery, but far less about the other industries in which enslaved people labored. This type of broad amnesia has narrowed and downplayed the contributions of the enslaved to society. For instance, antebellum southern ironworks employed about ten thousand enslaved workers, and more than thirty thousand worked in sugar refineries, rice mills, grist mills, and textile mills. Some industries employed both whites working for wages and enslaved blacks in the same factories and mills (Christian 1972; Dew 1966, 1994a, 1994b; Lewis 1979; Starobin 1970, 14–20). Jamie Brandon and James Davidson (2005, 113–131) refer to a form of industrial slavery at the Van Winkle Mill in the Ozark upland area of Arkansas. Slave labor also existed in the U.S. Armory at Harpers Ferry (Shackel and Larsen 2000). Even with this large presence, enslaved industrial workers go largely unacknowledged, partly because researchers have paid insufficient attention to labor, focusing instead on industrial development.

Similarly, the historical fact of slavery in the north, sometimes on northern plantations, but more often in other settings, surprises many people, partly because the limited scholarly research about it does not often reach the general public (figure 9.2). We purposefully highlight the work of non-academics in the following discussion. The investigative reporting of Anne Farrow, Joel

Figure 9.2   The African Burial Ground National Monument marks the site of a 6.6-acre burial ground in Lower Manhattan outside the boundaries of the settlement of New Amsterdam (now New York). At this site, from about the 1690s until 1794, both free and enslaved Africans were interred. The burial ground saw later landfill and development, but was rediscovered in 1991 as a result of the planned construction of a federal office building. (Image Courtesy of Kelly Fracchia.)

Long, and Jenifer Frank began with a story about the Hartford Courant's role in slavery, and expanded into a study of acts of complicity and profit making throughout the North. These three Northerners (Farrow et al. 2005, xix) speak for many Americans when they write: "We thought we knew our country. We were wrong."

Slavery supported the economic backbone of the whole country, north and south, intertwining commerce and violence in a remarkably persistent way. The story of direct participation and then complicity in slavery does not end with the Civil War. Farrow et al. (2005, 201) summarize by saying: "The Civil War ended slave labor in the United States, but not the idea that black people were inferior and inherently suited to physical labor, that they were made for exploitation and did not mind." American abolitionists' dreams of ending slavery did not extend outside the country's borders. Their book *Complicity: How the North Promoted, Prolonged, and Profited from Slavery* goes on to explore the horrors of enslavement of Africans in Africa for the exploitation of ivory, cloves, and sugar. Global connections apparent in the nineteenth century have, of course, continued to grow. Complicity with injustice for the sake of profit is still with us, cloaked in somewhat different issues, but still surrounding "outsiders" and labor. Slavery in our past is relevant to heritage work and to understanding the implications and lessons of history. Making the connections between past and present can help illuminate how slavery operates and how to eradicate such systemic exploitation.

From the earliest documented history of this country, those who controlled the economy and politics were concerned with the "immigrant problem," creating laws that dictated who and how many could enter the United States. Xenophobic fears had increased significantly by the end of the nineteenth and the beginning of the twentieth century. While we often understand that early immigrants toiled in poor working environments, we do not always recognize that new immigrants still face these conditions today. For instance, in New York City in the early twenty-first century, about 75 percent of those employed in garment factories are immigrants. The Labor Department considers approximately three-quarters of these work places to be sweatshops. Much like a century ago, people debate the ethics of sweatshop labor and discuss what should be done about these abuses. As soon as one sweatshop is closed by the Labor Department, another one appears in a different location with a ready workforce. The new immigrant is willing to work in substandard working conditions for below legal minimum wages because these places are often the best employment opportunity they have (Russell-Ciardi 2008:42; Ševčenko 2004).

In the United States, the Department of State estimates that 50,000 people are illegally trafficked into the country every year, and the total number of people enslaved in America is estimated at about 100,000 to 150,000. Sweatshops are the main place of business and many workers tend not to resist these conditions because the risk of legal action against sweatshop owners is small. The U.S. General Accounting Office defines sweatshops as "employers who violate more than one federal or state law governing minimum wage and overtime, child labor, industrial housework, occupational safety and health, workers' compensation, or industrial regulation" (Bales 2005, 93). Andrew Cockburn notes that these workers "live in fear of deportation" and "are cut off from any source of advice or support" (Chronicle of Higher Education 2003, B6).

In April 1998, the Smithsonian Institution took a daring step to address the issue of labor and exploitation with the opening of a temporary exhibit titled, "Between a Rock and a Hard Place: A History of American Sweatshops, 1820–present." The exhibit compared the history of labor with present realities. It introduced some of the important episodes of the history of sweatshops and the exhibit explained the nature of sweatshops in a globalized economy.

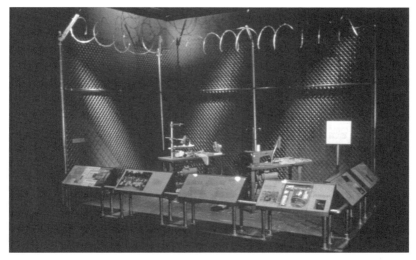

Figure 9.3   Re-created sewing machine workstations and interpretation of the El Monte sweatshop in the Sweatshops in America Exhibit at the National Museum of American History. (Image Courtesy of the Division of Work & Industry, National Museum of American History, Smithsonian Institution.)

A major part of the exhibit focused on an incident in El Monte, California, that served as an exposé of how sweatshops and slavery still exist in the United States (figure 9.3). In August 1995, federal and state police agents raided an apartment complex that was operating an illegal sweatshop. Young women from villages in Thailand had been deceived into coming to the United States to work in sweatshops. Ringleaders in their native land had recruited them with the promise of a better life, but when they arrived in the industrial compound, they were forced to work 16–18 hours a day for between $0.69 and $2.00 per hour (Saunders 1999). The garment workers sewed in virtual slavery for brand name clothing manufacturers and retailers. They were told that they would not be freed until they paid off the debt for their transportation to the United States. They also had to pay exorbitant prices for many of their necessities including toiletries and food. These workers were under constant surveillance, physically and verbally abused, and even threatened with rape and murder. Their housing conditions were overcrowded and unsanitary, and they were confined to their quarters with doors locked from the outside (Louie 2001). Guards stood outside of their quarters and a razor wire fence surrounded the compound (Bonacich and Appelbaum 2000; Liebhold and Rubenstein

2003; McGurrin 2007; Su 1997). When seventy-two Thai garment workers, mostly women, were freed from near-slavery, some had been there as long as seven years (McGurrin 2007:7; Su 1997). The uncovering of this sweatshop was newsworthy in the United States and startled most Americans, who generally believe that social reform and the labor movement have eradicated the phenomenon of sweatshops (National Museum of American History 1998).

Although the workers gained their freedom on August 2, 1995, they were imprisoned for nine days while the Immigration and Naturalization Service (INS) deliberated on their future. In 1996, they were granted legal residency with the right to work in the United States (Liebhold and Rubenstein 2003, 59–60; Louie 2001). The El Monte incident is probably the most visible and publicized violation of labor laws that has occurred in the United States. However, there are many other cases, and violations continue to occur. In the twenty-first century, the garment industry tends to be dominated by women workers. The conditions of exploitation and the threat of violence against these workers are widespread throughout the globe (Brooks 2007, xviii).

When visitors first entered the Smithsonian's "Between a Rock and a Hard Place" exhibit they were confronted with one of the most horrendous incidents in the history of the garment industry in the United States: the New York Triangle Shirtwaist Fire of 1911. In this tragic event, as a result of the common practice of management locking doors and exits in a factory, a fire killed over 140 immigrant workers, mostly women and girls, who could not escape the flames and smoke. This display was followed by one of a historic sweatshop as well as a reference to workers and their contributions to the war effort during World War II. Then came the shocking juxtaposition of past and present with a chain-link fence topped with barbed wire representing the El Monte incident.

The Smithsonian exhibit faced opposition from clothing manufacturers who tried to block its opening. This reaction led museums in San Francisco, Chicago, and New York to cancel the exhibit when it was scheduled to travel later that year. In November 1999, the exhibit opened in the Simon Wiesenthal Center's Museum of Tolerance, located on the edge of Beverly Hills. At the opening, Liebe Geft, the museum director, explained to his audience, "Sometimes we have to look at the very stark and extreme examples to arouse us into a readiness to engage in debate" (quoted in Liebhold and Rubenstein 2003, 70). On a Sunday in January 2000, a large number of Thai and Latino garment workers used their day off to see their own story featured in the exhibit. The museum organized a reception for the El Monte workers and honored their struggle for justice. Julie Su, an Asian Pacific American Legal Center Attorney, described them as heroes, saying, "You have stirred so many people from apathy and ignorance" (quoted in Liebhold and Rubenstein 2003, 57).

An increase in sweatshops in the United States is directly related to the globalization of our economy and to Americans' desire for unrealistically cheap goods. Manufacturers are looking for new ways to decrease costs in order to maintain or increase market demand. Some of the abuses in the garment industry have occurred in U.S. territories, which allow companies to apply the label "Made in the USA." The Commonwealth of the Northern Mariana Islands (CNMI) is one of these territories. The CNMI, which consists of fourteen islands, is located in Micronesia in the western Pacific Ocean. As a result of World War II, the United Nations combined the Micronesian Islands with the Mariana Islands to form the Trust Territory of the Pacific Islands (TTPI). The United States agreed to be the trustee. In the late 1960s, the islands of the TTPI discussed the nature of their relationship with the United States. While many of the islands wanted more independence, the Mariana Islands decided on a closer relationship with the United States. The Northern Mariana Islands voted to become a U.S. commonwealth in 1975, and in 1976, Congress approved this status (Cruz Cuison 2000, 67). Inhabitants of the Northern Mariana Island became U.S. citizens, although governed by their own constitution.

Until recently, the U.S. Immigration and Nationality Act and the federal minimum wage provision of the Fair Labor and Standards Act did not apply in the CNMI. This exemption was part of the agreement that created the relationship between the Marianas and the United States. These exemptions led to significant economic development, as well as a dramatic influx of workers who were exploited, cheated, and indentured. The garment industry, nonexistent in the early 1980s, quickly developed as the Commonwealth's major industry (Cruz Cuison 2000, 63–64, 71). Enforcing federal labor laws is difficult since the main office is thousands of miles away. The owner of several garment factories also owned the largest newspaper, so it was difficult to report on labor injustices.

Because of loopholes in U.S. immigration and wage laws as well and generally poor enforcement, Asian-based garment manufacturers flocked to the Commonwealth along with tens of thousands of foreign- speaking indentured workers. Non–English speakers were seen as a benefit to the textile industry since they were less apt to file a complaint. Foreign workers, lured by the prospect of good U.S. jobs, outnumbered native workers. The Commonwealth admitted immigrants as temporary workers, under a law that limited work contracts to one year. However, foreign workers paid an exorbitant recruitment fee that would take several years to pay off. They signed contracts that waived several basic human rights, preventing them from joining a union, striking, attending religious services, marrying, or resigning. As a result of their large debts, workers were dependent on their jobs, and they were under great pressure to remain silent about the abusive working conditions (Bales 2005:96-97).

The textile workers labored seventy to eighty hours per week without overtime pay. Their housing conditions were squalid and unsanitary. They lived in crowded company owned barracks, for which they paid up to $200 a month in room and board. Meanwhile, loopholes in the labor laws allowed textile manufacturers to pay below minimum wages (at the time $3.05 per hour or $488 per month). At the same time, their products bore the label, "Made in the USA."

Apologists for sweatshops argue that the global apparel trade will bring economic development to the poor regions of the world through better employment and increased wages. While many factory owners compete for orders with low bids, the low bids make it easier to allow abuses. The welfare of workers is often overlooked. It is the factory owner who dictates the terms of employment, which allows for low wages and weak or no enforcement of local labor laws. Much about these current labor situations and the growth of sweatshops forces us to question whether wealth actually trickles down the economic ladder in developing countries (Rosen 2002, 5; Ross 2004).

In 1997, Rep. Tom DeLay, (R-TX), the House majority whip at the time, visited the Commonwealth on New Year's Eve. As a guest of the CNMI government, he stated that he would fight any federal takeover of Saipan's immigration and labor laws. ABC-TV News recorded DeLay telling his host, "You are a shining light for what is happening in the Republican Party, and you represent everything that is good about what we are trying to do in America and leading the world in the free-market system" (Shields 1998, A7). In 1998, Rep. George Miller, (D-CA) visited the Saipan factories in the CNMI, and later introduced legislation to raise the minimum wage and impose federal control of immigration. The *Seattle Post-Intelligencer* (Shields1998, A7) reported that Miller had little success as part of the House minority. It was almost a decade before this legislation passed in the fall of 2007.

In 2007, local control of the minimum wage was superseded by the U. S. Congress. For over a decade the minimum hourly wage in the Commonwealth had been $3.05. After 2007, the local minimum wage was to be increased by $0.50 per hour annually in order to catch up with the U.S. standard (Vallejera 2007). In May 2008, Congress passed a law mandating that U.S. immigration laws apply to the CNMI, and that they supersede and replace all local immigration laws. Transition to U.S. immigration laws began on November 28, 2009 (Misulich 2011). All of these changes and government regulations put the Commonwealth garment industry under severe economic pressure and many garment factories have since closed (de la Torre 2007).

At one time, enslavement was sanctioned by governments. Today, it is illegal everywhere although it still exists, and its forms have changed from what we know about it historically. When we connect the history of labor and migration to contemporary issues, we discover uncomfortable continuities, particularly that of complicity. Raising consciousness awakens us to an awareness of injustices and inequalities that exist worldwide. Andrew Cockburn notes that there are estimates that about twenty-seven million people in the world are enslaved, in the sense that they are "physically confined or restrained and forced to work, or controlled through violence, or in some way treated as property" (Chronicle of Higher Education 2003, B6; Bales 2005, 4). The enslaved person is denied all of his or her freedoms for the economic gain of someone else. The majority of bonded labor, where people enter into debt bondage to secure against a loan or an inherited debt, occurs in India, Pakistan, Bangladesh, and Nepal (Bales 2004, 9). Enslavement is a global phenomenon; it has been documented in just about every country in the world (9). Because of a global population boom, coupled with extreme poverty and urbanization, the cost of enslaving people is cheaper than it has ever been. In many areas, slavery no longer involves a large capital purchase, such as might be necessary for livestock. This phenomenon means that the enslaved are more likely to be seen as disposable. In many instances, contemporary enslavement tends not to be a life-long condition; it may last only a few years, and in some cases for a even shorter time.

These changes in enslavement can also be discerned in the changing definitions of slavery as proclaimed in different slavery conventions from the early twentieth century. The 1926 Slavery Convention, under the auspices of the League of Nations, defined the condition as "forced labor." The UN Universal Declaration of Human Rights in 1948 added "servitude" to the definition.

The 1956 UN Supplementary Convention further noted servile status as that which includes debt bondage, serfdom, unfree marriage, and the exploitation of young people for their labor. The Rome Final Act of the International Criminal Court in 1998 also included trafficking as a form of enslavement (Bales 2005, 51).

The old system of slavery is very much part of history and part of the U.S. historical consciousness. In that system, one person legally owned another person, and that type of slavery was abolished long ago. However, a new system of slavery continues in which bonded labor exists in many different forms, even though it is illegal. Contemporary labor injustices, immigration, human trafficking, and enslavement still exist today. While we may feel comfortable discussing the historical context of these issues, it is also important to move out of our comfort zone and connect these issues to the present, even when it becomes politically dangerous to do so as we confront the hidden realities of a global economy. Lest we think that these labor injustices are in the past, in April 2013, a garment building collapsed in Bangladesh, killing 1132 garment workers. Few building codes existed, and the owner ignored others. That factory manufactured many garments for multinational American apparel stores (Uddin 2013).

The National Underground Railroad Freedom Center is located in Cincinnati, Ohio, on the Ohio River across from Covington, Kentucky (figure 9.4). The Ohio River and the city of Cincinnati were important destinations for enslaved people who were striving to emancipate themselves by journeying north into free states. This museum tells the historical story of the Underground Railroad as a struggle for freedom and explicitly connects that story to the reality of slavery today. On their website (http://www.freedomcenter.org) the museum describes its mission as a site of conscience: "We reveal stories about freedom's heroes, from the era of the Underground Railroad to contemporary times, challenging and inspiring everyone to take courageous steps for freedom today". Such museums are the pioneers of the next generation of museums, historically rooted and focused on the consequences of our legacies.

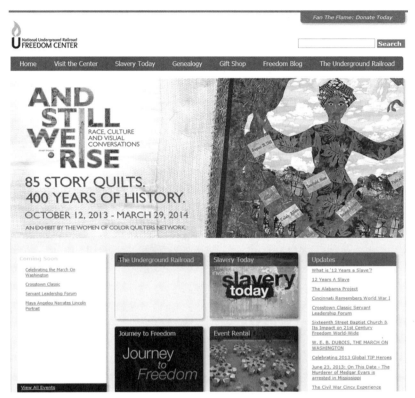

Figure 9.4   National Underground Railroad Freedom Center website at   http://freedomcenter.org/.

Chapter 10

Museums and Civic Engagement

The Leading Role of Museums in Civic Engagement

The American Alliance of Museums (AAM) (formerly the American Association of Museums) has called on museums and historic places that convey local
or global heritage to become places of learning where people can use lessons
from the past to address contemporary political and social issues. Making
these links between the past and the present can facilitate an exploration of
both historic and contemporary concerns related to social justice (American
Association of Museums 2002).

The AAM has continued to promote civic engagement initiatives and to
take a leadership role in confronting the implications of issues of demographic
diversity for museum visitation. There is no question that the U.S. population
is changing. By about 2050, African Americans, Latinos (of any race), Asian
Americans and Pacific Islanders, Native Americans, as well as those who identify as multiracial, will collectively become the new majority. While the country
is becoming more ethnically diverse, the people who visit cultural places such
as museums do not necessarily reflect this. The National Endowment for the
Arts *Survey of Public Participation in the Arts* published in June 2009, shows
that non-Hispanic white Americans, though making up 68.7 percent of the U.S.
population, accounted for 78.9 percent of the adult art museum visitors in 2008
(Farrell and Medvedeva 2010, 9–13). Hispanics and African Americans were
significantly underrepresented. The gap between the percentage of white and
non-white Americans who visit art museums has grown steadily since the first

survey was conducted in 1982. On a similar note, a survey conducted by the Institute of Museum and Library Services found Asian Americans to have the highest participation rates for art museums (36.6 percent) and for science and technology museums (34.1 percent). Whites had the highest visitor rates in historic houses or sites (37.3 percent) and history museums (24.3 percent). Hispanics had the highest attendance rates at natural history museums (25.3 percent). African Americans had the lowest participation rates (ranging from 18 to 22 percent) across all categories of museum types.

Many professionals in the museum world, as well as those connected to the interpretation of historic places, find such evidence as troubling, especially if low visitation by non-whites persists. Therefore, the AAM is beginning to ask important questions: Why do some groups not use museums? What can museums do to become a vital part of the lives of people they do not serve now? What more can they do to alter this alarming trend? (Farrell and Medvedeva 2010, 9–13). It is clear that each museum needs to understand the community in which it operates, and recognize the social, political, and economic contexts in which it exists.

It becomes important for museums to break down barriers and develop different strategies to reach out to their constituencies. Many museums rise to the challenge by working with local ethnic communities to bridge differences and become viable centers for discourse on issues that are important and relevant to communities. Some museums explicitly create safe spaces and foster dialogue about race, ethnicity, immigration, and culture. Culturally specific museums that attempt to break down their traditional boundaries and explore similarities and differences between groups have provided a new way of making important links to different groups. For example, the curators at the National Museum of Mexican Art in Chicago worked with members of the local Latino and African American communities to develop an exhibition titled: "The African Presence in Mexico: From Yanga to the Present." This work heightened the community's awareness about the complex history of race and ethnicity in Mexico. In Seattle, the Wing Luke Asian Museum serves as a cultural center for the Asian Pacific American communities (figure 10.1). Its goal is to promote cross-cultural understanding among the many different groups and nationalities that are categorized as "Asian," promoting the idea that there are many different groups that fall into this category, each with their own distinctive cultural norms and values (Farrell and Medvedeva 2010, 20).

The Levine Museum of the New South in Charlotte, North Carolina, responded to a finding in Robert Putnam's report on social capital that identi-

Figure 10.1 Interior of the Yick Fung Company, which is part of the Wing Luke Museum, Seattle, WA. (Photograph by Paul A. Shackel.)

fied Charlotte as having a low level of intergroup trust. The museum developed exhibitions specifically around issues of race, racism, and trust. In 2004, its first effort to address the issue of trust was titled "Courage." The exhibition addressed the history of school desegregation. Working with a community group, the museum brought in professionals from across the city to develop focused discussions on this topic. Betty Farrell and Maria Medvedeva (2010, 20) identify what made this project engaging: "The hallmarks of the project are engaging and provocative questions that get people talking about tough issues: Who judges you without knowing you? Who do you judge? What parts of your cultural heritage have you kept? Let go of? What cultural aspects of the South most surprised you?" The museum used a historical event to develop a deeper understanding of some of the contemporary challenges that face the community. Due to the success of the exhibition, which acted as a catalyst for community dialogue, the commitment to community is now an important part of the museum's mission. The Levine Museum of the New South has taken a leadership role in their region for developing civic programs that address demographic changes.

The museum community continues its active self-reflection. In 2009, the Institute of Museum and Library Services culminated a dialogue among practitioners with a report called "The Future of Museums and Libraries: A

Discussion Guide" (Pastore 2009). They focused their dialogue on "changing conceptions of institutional authority, relationships between institution and audience, tools and modes of communication, knowledge transfer, information exchange and professional practice" tempered by the ongoing responsibility to "preserve and make accessible tangible and intangible original material remains" (Pastore 2009, 4). The discussion guide is designed to provoke further communication about roles and relationships among these institutions and society. The resulting questions ask us to think about the roles of museums and libraries in the context of twenty-first-century society:

- How can such places engage public interest, insight and action?

- Foster democracy?

- Strive for social justice?

There are, of course, a wide variety of types of cultural events and of museums and historic places. We can learn a great deal from each other, especially about social responsibility.

Many heritage professions are engaging in similar self-reflection with the purpose of becoming more relevant and sustainable. The American Association for State and Local History, the National Trust for Historic Preservation, the American Association of Museums, and the American Architectural Foundation cosponsored a summit at Kykuit (the historic Rockefeller estate in Westchester, New York) on the sustainability of historic sites (Vogt 2007, and see Doyle 2012). The summit, which focused on transforming historic sites through their relationships with and service to local communities, produced the findings and recommendations reproduced here in table 10.1.

The Kykuit findings (see Vogt 2007) reject tourism as a viable path to sustainability, and focus instead on serving the needs of the local community. For example, one finding is that, "Sustainability begins with each historic site's engagement with its community and its willingness to change its structure, programs, and services in response to the changing needs of that community." Some of the recommendations that build on such findings include:

- "The profession must develop new measures, beyond attendance, that document the quality of visitor engagement at sites and extend community outreach beyond the bounds of the historic site."

- "Historic sites must no longer think of the 'velvet rope tour' as their basic 'bread and butter' program and must generate more varied ways to utilize their remarkable resources to enrich people's lives."

- "The historic site community must reaffirm the importance of these places for our nation's future and redefine their mission, in terms of that future rather than the past."

Museums are working to become vital and relevant members of civically engaged communities. It is not just large or prominent museums that are undertaking this re-invention, but the local and often traditional museums are doing so as well.

Historic House Museums

Estimates of the number of historic house museums in the United States range between 6,000 and 15,000—there are a lot of these places (Doyle 2012). It started to become apparent in the 1990s that financial sustainability was becoming a real challenge for these sites. Visitation continues to decrease, partly attributed to the lure of technology and other, more active, recreational destinations. But decreasing visitation and relevance are also attributed to changing national demographics, in terms of both age and ethnic or racial identity. The trend in the United States toward a majority minority population combined with relatively low visitor numbers among non-whites fuels many museums' anxiety about their relevance and survival.

Faced with uncertain futures, some historic house museums have been following the lead of the broader museum community in using civic engagement and other techniques to re-invent themselves. Practitioners at these sites have been striving to find, create, or co-create relevancy among their constituencies. These museums recognize the need to make the transition from a focus on the furnishings to a focus on relevant issues rooted in the past. Figures 10.2–10.8 highlight a handful of museums taking this approach.

Reinventing the purpose of heritage work requires that we take seriously the demands of practicing antiracism and antidiscrimination. Such as stance requires more than trying to eliminate biases from our work, it requires active engagement against the structures of oppression interwoven throughout our society. The scope of our activist ambitions may change from project to project, but each concerns the intersections among ethics, activism, politics, and responsibility.

TABLE 10.1   FINDINGS AND RECOMMENDATIONS OF THE 2007 KYKUIT SUMMIT (REPRODUCED FROM VOGT 2007 [NUMBERS ADDED])

Findings

1. Successful stewardship of the nation's historic sites requires financial sustainability.

2. Sustainability begins with each historic site's engagement with the community and its willingness to change its structure, programs, and services in response to the changing needs of the community.

3. The long-accepted tourism business model is not a sustainable business model for most historic sites.

4. Serving the needs of the local community (not the tourist audience) is the most valuable and most sustainable goal for most historic sites.

5. Attendance figures are not the most valid measure of the positive value and impact of the historic house experience.

6. Many professional standards and practices in the historic site field were borrowed from the museum community and, in practice, often deter creativity and sustainability at historic sites.

7. New standards of stewardship for historic sites should be modeled to reflect the distinct nature of these places.

8. Responsible site stewardship achieves a sustainable balance between the needs of the buildings, landscapes, collections, and the visiting public.

9. The buildings, landscapes, and collections are the means but not the ends of the work of historic sites.

10. Innovation, experimentation, collaboration, and a broad sharing of the resulting information are essential to achieving historic site sustainability on a broad scale.

11. Undefined collecting, coupled with professional standards and practices regarding deaccessioning, are impediments to change and sustainability.

12. Program, challenge, and matching grants can reduce long-term sustainability by shifting focus away from operating and endowment needs and by encouraging the growth of non-mission-related programs.

13. Returning sites to private ownership with proper easements can be a positive means of assuring long-term stewardship.

Lori Stahlgren (2012) describes some of the changes that archaeology has helped to bring about at a historic site in Louisville, Kentucky. The name change from Farmington Historic Home to Farmington Historic Plantation, broadens the story beyond the mansion's white inhabitants to include the enslaved who lived and worked on the same land (figures 10.9 and 10.10). The archaeology done there has been instrumental in changing the interpretation and educational programs because it has focused on slavery. Stahlgren (2012:108) reflects that:

TABLE 10.1   FINDINGS AND RECOMMENDATIONS OF THE 2007 KYKUIT SUMMIT (REPRODUCED FROM VOGT 2007 [NUMBERS ADDED]) (CONTINUED)

Recommendations

1. The [American Association for State and Local History] AASLH Task Force on Standards should seek to establish and appropriate stewardship balance for the needs of buildings, landscapes, collections, and the public.

2. The AASLH Ethics Committee should prepare a positive statement to guide the transitioning of historic sites and returning them to private stewardship.

3. The National Trust and others should experiment with responsible situational standards for collections, buildings, and landscapes at pilot sites that could serve as models for others, and they should publish their findings as appropriate.

4. Foundations and granting agencies should refocus their philanthropy away from short-term program support to grants that assist sites in building their capacity to sustain themselves for the long term, including GOS [General Operating Support] and endowment.

5. Foundations should be supported in their efforts to terminate repeated "drip support" to historic sites to focus their support on sties taking positive steps to achieve long-term sustainability.

6. Those who educate and develop the leadership of historic sites should amend their curricula to better equip students to deal successfully with rapidly changing realities.

7. The major professional associations should encourage, promote, publicize, and recognize experimental and successful models of change and sustainable practices.

8. The profession must develop new measures, beyond attendance, that document the quality of visitor engagement at sites and the extent of community outreach beyond the bounds of the historic site.

9. Historic sites must no longer think of the "velvet rope tour" as their basic "bread and butter" program and must generate more varied ways to utilize their remarkable resources to enrich people's lives.

10. The historic site community must reaffirm the importance of these places for our nation's future and redefine their mission, in terms of that future rather than the past.

11. Selected sites should develop a pilot process to streamline deaccessioning.

When archaeologists originally planned the excavations at Farmington in 1997, they did not realize that the focus they gave to slavery would ignite a debate about Louisville's slave past as it reflects the racial tensions of the present. They did not consider that they would be dealing with the remnants of the festering racial wounds of slavery. Today, this has changed. Archaeology, both the process and the product, is used as an instrument to foster a discussion of the history.

Figure 10.2   The Botto National Historic Landmark in Haledon, NJ, is home to the American Labor Museum, which commemorates the history and meaning of work and labor. It interprets the labor movement throughout the world, with special attention to the ethnicity and immigrant experience of American workers. It also provides a variety of labor education programs for union apprentices to explore historic workers' struggles and contemporary issues of the labor movement. (http://www.labormuseum.net/. Image courtesy of American Labor Museum/Botto House National Landmark.)

Figure 10.3   Teachers attending the American Labor Museum's annual teachers' workshop, whose objective is to introduce methods of integrating labor and immigrant studies into the curriculum. (Image Courtesy of American Labor Museum/Botto House National Landmark).

Figure 10.4   The Matilda Joslyn Gage House in Fayetteville, NY, is dedicated to educating current and future generations to drive contemporary social change. Gage was a progressive visionary who, with Elizabeth Cady Stanton and Susan B. Anthony, organized the political action of the nineteenth-century women's suffrage movement in the United States. The historic house's website declares that "You will quickly discover that this place is not just one more dusty museum where you see how an important person lived. It is a museum of conscience in community, where the vision of human freedom and democracy that fired Matilda Joslyn Gage 150 years ago speaks to the present and resonates into the future." (http://www.matildajoslyngage.org/. Image courtesy of Patricia Campany.)

The museum has changed the way it interacts with both its various histories and its publics. These changes were encouraged by the archaeologists who worked to uncover some of the long-silenced past.

Archaeology at historic house museums can be powerful, but it is not enough, as there are many places never recognized or curated as places important enough to preserve. Heritage also exists in places where museums do not because stories were thought to be unimportant or legacies were erased intentionally or through neglect.

Figure 10.5   Cliveden in Philadelphia, PA, is a historic mansion that was the scene
of some of the bloodiest fighting during the Battle of Germantown in 1777. It tells
the story of American identity through four centuries of changing political, gender,
racial, ethnic, religious, and class identities from the American Revolution through
the struggle for emancipation. Cliveden has a formal relationship with the organization Historians Against Slavery, which is a coalition of scholars, museums, activists,
and concerned citizens who draw connections between the historical enslavement
of African Americans and modern day human trafficking. (http://www.cliveden.org/
discover. Image courtesy of Cliveden, a National Trust Historic Site.)

Archaeology can de-silence people, places, and stories that have been
made to disappear through willful destruction or neglect. As has been so
powerfully demonstrated in countries all over the world, forensic archaeology reclaims victims from disappearance. This reclaiming is something that
archaeology can do particularly well. It can point to the evidence, the reality, of
people's lives on the landscape and in the domestic spaces. Archaeology helps
mark reality on the ground.

The curation of buildings, structures, and landscapes as tangible remains
of the past often ignores the presence and power of the archaeological record.
Consider the Kykuit summit's findings and recommendations cited earlier.
Even as historic preservationists consider the need to expand their discipline's
relevance and to serve and to open dialogues with long-marginalized communities, they continue to be devoted to sustaining remnants of the status quo of
privileged places and groups.

Figure 10.6 Paulsdale, the former home of Alice Paul in Mount Laurel, New Jersey, was designated a National Historic Landmark in 1991. It is managed by the Alice Paul Institute, which was founded in 1984 by a group of dedicated volunteers to commemorate the centennial of Alice Paul's 1885 birth and to further her legacy. Alice Paul dedicated her life to securing equal rights for all women in the early twentieth century. Her life symbolizes the long struggle for justice in the United States and around the world. She believed that women and men should be equal partners in society. The mission of the Alice Paul Institute is to promote full gender equality through education, development, and empowerment of leaders, and it strives to develop future generations of leaders and human rights activists. (http://alicepaul.org/api.htm. Image courtesy of the Alice Paul Institute.)

In his often-cited treatise on historical silencing, Michel-Rolph Trouillot (1995) contrasts two common meanings of history—one as the past and the other as stories about the past—and observes how power creates both narratives and silences. Trouillot (1995, 115) writes: "The power to decide what is trivial—and annoying—is also part of the power to decide how 'what happened' becomes 'that which is said to have happened.'" Archaeology at, and of, places that are already recognized and commemorated as "historic" is often important for telling more inclusive histories of such places because material remains matter.

Figure 10.7   The Harriet Beecher Stowe Center in Hartford, CT, uses its historic house museum for community building and problem solving. In 1852, Harriet Beecher Stowe wrote Uncle Tom's Cabin, a remarkably influential book that roused public passion for the abolition of slavery prior to the American Civil War. The center has built on the legacy of its namesake with tours and programs encouraging the public to take action for social justice. Here Katherine D. Kane, Stowe Center Executive Director, is shown at the July 2013 Salon at Stowe workshop "How To Fight Intolerance," with Dr. William Howe of the Connecticut Department of Education. (http://HarrietBeecherStowe.org. Image courtesy of Harriet Beecher Stowe Center.)

Why Visit a Museum or Historic Site?

What does the heritage worker at a historic site want from a visitor? In the context of informal education, the National Association for Interpretation seeks to offer opportunities for visitors to make their own personal intellectual and emotional connections to places. The mission of the Smithsonian Institution focuses on the "increase and diffusion of knowledge." Museum educators want visitors to learn, and museums seek to engage and involve visitors in creating meaning.

Museum experts who study the ways that visitors move through exhibits often are disappointed with how little time people actually spend reading and looking, a frustration that has given rise to lots of proposals about how to engage the visitor and improve museum education. But it is not necessarily the

Figure 10.8   Bowne House in Flushing, NY, was the home of John Bowne. Teresa Moyer (2004) designed an education program for the Bowne House to celebrate John Bowne's seventeenth-century activities in defense of religious liberty. Moyer sought to tap into the longer historical continuum represented by archaeology to give local students and teachers more tools with which to explore the urban change in their own community. Students use maps, historical documents, and archaeological collections as primary documents to consider tolerance, social change, and civic responsibility. (http://bownehouse.org/. Image courtesy of APdP2 Studios, Bowne House Historical Society.)

case that people are going to museums to learn new things. Jay Rounds (2006) has made a compelling argument that as visitors we go to museums partly to do identity work: that is, at least partly to reinforce what we think we know about how the world works and our place in it. We also go to do some identity exploration, to try out different perspectives while in the safe environment of a place that demands no commitments. We do such exploration to feed our psychological need to prepare for the future just in case it is not exactly like the present. This identity work can be done very quickly, as it is not necessary to read or learn many specific details in a history museum to have one's assumptions about orderly cause and effect confirmed. Those of us who have spent a lot of time in house museums cannot help but notice a remarkable sameness

Figure 10.9   Farmington Historic Plantation house, Louisville, KY. (Image courtesy of Farmington Historic Plantation Collection.)

to the metanarratives that structure those experiences. If you are comfortable with those structures, then the museums can be comforting and affirming. And, if you are not, perhaps you stay away.

Rounds (133) contends that visitors use museums to do their own identity work. He contrasts this function with the apparent lack of learning that worries museum professionals, as research on visitor behavior shows that most people simply skim their way through exhibits. Museum educators conclude that because they spend an inadequate amount of time reading text and observing objects, visitors are not learning adequately and are not engaged in the museum's messages. Identity work, however, lends itself to such partial use of exhibits. While Rounds' analysis is focused on visitation to traditional museums, it is not much of a stretch to apply it as well to historic house museums and other historic places that allow visitation.

One of the characteristics of museums that Rounds believes visitors use in this identity work is an intensified sense of order, which supports stability and security. Offering a reassuring order drawn from the chaos of history is one of the most striking functions of traditional historic places. Such places adopt and impose order on the past by identifying certain places and stories

Figure 10.10   A Farmington Historic Plantation house interpreter works with two visitors. (Image courtesy of Farmington Historic Plantation.)

worthy of preservation, establishing acceptable and unsurprising metanarratives about cause and effect, and labeling in a way that reflects certain underlying social hierarchies of professional, amateur, and general public.

Given that visitors will always bring themselves and their needs and stories about their own identities with them, what is the role for the socially conscious heritage worker? Identity work is not only about stability; less frequently, but potentially more intensely, it is also about change. Rounds is in agreement with his colleagues that transformative experiences in museums will be very rare, although certain high-impact historical events lend themselves to enabling such experiences. Instead of seeking to transform visitors, he suggests that museums should recognize that visitors use museums to build their own capacities for transformation that may or may not happen. "Identity exploration" provides a safe way to try out other ideas, other ways of being. However, visitors may simultaneously be collecting potential alternative ideas, even as they maintain their identities by confirming what they already "know" about the world. This can happen whether it is explicit or implicit in the exhibits and presentations they experience.

There are some implications for historic places, of course. As discussed earlier, the demography of the United States is changing rapidly. The self-identified white majority is losing what appeared to be a stable part of American identity. The historical creation of a "white" identity has not often been part of the structural story explicitly told in American historic places. If structural and cultural violence rooted in ideas about white supremacy are to be confronted, then the story needs to be clearly and completely told in ways that will be heard.

Heritage places provide a particularly rich source of alternative stories and alternative identity. As Rounds (2006, 146) observes that, "Before change can occur, it is necessary to reach a state in which one can imagine the possibility that things might be different from the way we believe them to be now." Identity, as we are aware through experience, can become a remarkably contentious point of conflict when it is threatened. It is one of the most intractable of issues in conflict resolution. Identity struggles are often implicated in active violent conflict and in structural and cultural violence, so we know that identity work is socially and culturally important. When heritage analysts point out time and again that heritage is contested discourse, they frequently note that identity is the main cause. Remember Gable's observations about Monticello? That it functions as an inadvertent shrine to white identity provides an example of the embedded and frequently unconscious messages at heritage sites.

Heritage professions need people with diverse backgrounds and viewpoints to identify and uncover the structures of both textual and material culture narratives. This work must be intentional and tireless, and be done with a powerful, albeit difficult, mixture of passion and humility. Revealing the structure of the narrative and the stories leads to revealing the sources and the work that these narratives do in the world, whether that work is to perpetuate inequalities or to reassert the human dignity of a particular group.

Sites of Conscience

The International Coalition of Sites of Conscience (originally the International Coalition of Historic Sites of Conscience) sets the gold standard for relevance and social responsibility for historic places. The Coalition is a network of historic places committed to addressing contemporary legacies of past struggles whose mission statement reads: "We are sites, individuals, and initiatives activating the power of places of memory to engage the public in connecting past and present in order to envision and shape a more just and humane future"

(International Coalition of Sites of Conscience 2012). In 1999, nine institutions from four continents formed the Coalition with the belief "that it is the
obligation of historic sites to assist the public in drawing connections between
the history of our sites and its contemporary implications. We view stimulating
dialogue on pressing social issues and promoting democratic and humanitarian values as a primary function" (Ševčenko and Russell-Ciardi 2008, 9–10).
The challenge is to encourage historic places to engage local communities in
issues that matter most to them, thereby encouraging the democratic process.

Although the Coalition dropped "historic" from its name, it defines sites
of conscience as institutions that "interpret history through historic sites; engage in programs that stimulate dialogue on pressing social issues; promote
humanitarian and democratic values as a primary function; and share opportunities for public involvement in issues raised at the site." There are seventeen
founding sites and hundreds of members, including many of the museums we
have mentioned in this chapter. The practice shared among the sites for interpreting critical issues is a facilitated dialogue, along the lines of the dialogue
strategy we discussed in chapter 5 as central to public deliberation and the
working through of social issues.

The work of one of the founding members—the Lower East Side Tenement Museum in New York City—connects past and present through the lens-
es of labor and migration (http://www.tenement.org). The museum preserves
a five-story building that was home to over 7,000 immigrants from more than
20 different nationalities between 1863 and 1935, and it makes immigrant history socially relevant. As an Affiliated Area of the National Park Service, it
is associated with Ellis Island and Castle Clinton. The museum's mission is,
"to promote tolerance and historical perspective through the presentation and
interpretation of the variety of immigrant and migrant experiences on Manhattan's Lower East Side, a gateway to America." Visitors can engage in discussions about the human rights issues the new Americans faced—including
labor exploitation; gender, racial and ethnic discrimination; and poverty—all
issues that are relevant to new immigrants today. Community organizations
serving immigrant residents have collaborated with the museum on program-
ming that uses history to orient and inspire new immigrant populations. Visitors have opportunities to learn about the experiences of immigration and, in
the process, identify with those experiences. Those involved in the museum
believe that historical discussions of the immigrant experience can create a
sense of empathy and tolerance for the new immigrant (Russell-Ciardi 2008,

42; Ševčenko 2004). Furthermore, they recognize that the immigrant experience is one condition that helps unite people across time and culture.

Connecting the past and the present along with the local and the global through shared stories provides some of the most powerful tools we have for raising consciousness and encouraging public engagement with ongoing, historically rooted, critical issues.

PART THREE

Story of Now

Stories of self comprise the *story of us* with shared meanings and goals. The *story of now* tells how we, as a collaborative of practitioners in many fields, translate our shared ideas and ambitions into actions, not in the undefined future, but now.

Heritage is part of the consciousness raising necessary for any of us to understand the ways in which the past weighs on the present. Heritage workers are convinced that heritage places and heritage stories do real work in society, ranging widely from reinforcing to challenging and overturning structural bias and cultural violence.

We propose reframing heritage as healing, rather than as conflict. We do not propose this to deflect or diminish analysis of serious and violent legacies of heritage. We propose this as a shift of intention, from analysis as an endpoint toward analysis as a foundation for advocacy, for justice, and for peacebuilding.

To do this reframing requires intentionality. We can be intentional about deep analysis of our stories, about raising consciousness, and, perhaps most difficult, about helping in the working through needed to learn from the past to solve problems of now. Heritage workers will need to do considerable working through of our own challenges to figure out how to participate effectively in public problem solving using our expertise tempered by an appropriate sense of humility.

We propose that heritage workers from any discipline begin thinking of ourselves primarily as members of the public. That is, we believe that heritage workers will have a seat at the table of public deliberation when we pull up a chair alongside everyone else and lend our expertise in a spirit of collaboration and problem solving. Many perspectives are needed to understand and meet collective challenges. We will be more effective and our skills are more likely to be helpful if we do not come to the table as experts to whom others should defer, but as members

Archaeology, Heritage, and Civic Engagement, Barbara J. Little and Paul A. Shackel, p. 145–146.

of society with skills and knowledge along with big gaps in our knowledge and understanding that we rely on others to fill.

Heritage is an essential part of civil society. It is not separate and we, as practitioners, are simply members of the public, regardless of how we earn our living. We live on our earth. We live in our societies. Our problems are shared problems.

Chapter 11

Building Peace Through Heritage

A Heritage-based Peacebuilding Model

We want to offer some observations and suggestions about making connections between heritage practices in historic places and alternative approaches to conflict resolution. Kevin Avruch (2012) describes how the practice of conflict resolution has grown in scope. The field has been increasingly influenced by the field of peace studies, whose practitioners have characterized traditional conflict resolution as overly pragmatic, blind to structural violence, and unconcerned with social justice and stable peace. Practitioners of alternative approaches to conflict resolution are seeking change by moving away from a focus on postconflict and toward a focus on building peace and peaceful relationships based on justice and reconciliation. This trend leads toward goals of permanently altering relationships and radically empowering those who have suffered. Such work is more accurately thought of as positive peacebuilding rather than traditional conflict resolution, but the language of these approaches appears to remain somewhat fluid.

Avruch characterizes the cultural turn in conflict resolution and summarizes three alternative approaches—transformative, narrative, and insight—each of which is termed a type of mediation. Dialogue and mediated conversation are techniques common to these alternative approaches, which are focused more on healing relationships than on settling the classic buyer-seller interaction. This latter buyer-seller model is a transactional model based on

Archaeology, Heritage, and Civic Engagement, Barbara J. Little and Paul A. Shackel, p. 147–154.

negotiating interests, popularized in the influential best seller, *Getting to Yes,* originally published in 1981 (Fisher et al. 2011).

There are certain common skills needed in each of the three approaches. These include listening and careful questioning, awareness of power and other relational dynamics, and close attention to narratives. Transformative mediation views conflict as a symptom of a deeper crisis of human interaction and focuses on realigning and balancing distorted relationships. It is meant to allow parties to recognize the destructive aspects of their conflict, get past crisis, and explore terms of resolution.

Narrative mediation pays close attention to stories by which people live their lives. The mediator draws out stories with the aim of deconstructing them to unmask power or other destructive elements and then works with parties to co-author new narratives that demand a change in thinking. Questioning and deconstruction replaces traditional analysis and problem solving with the goal of de-authorizing some stories and encouraging a discursive shift to alternative, non-conflictual stories.

Insight mediation is based on values and a four-step model of learning comprising experience, understanding, judgment, and decision. Experience is gained by gathering and absorbing information, which leads to understanding. One needs understanding in order to achieve the insight required for the third step of judgment. Subsequently, this cumulative learning results in decisions, and then actions.

We are less concerned with choosing a particular form of alternative conflict resolution then with a blended approach that makes sense for heritage work. Purists may object to the way we are conflating these alternatives. However, their common skills are those also required for effective collaboration and for the "working through" necessary for coming to public judgment. Therefore, we advocate exploration and experimentation with any peacebuilding approach, and we believe that each of these approaches has something to offer heritage workers who are reinventing their historic places as sites focused on the needs of communities and addressing the problems they face.

We want to offer a heritage-based peacebuilding model that considers heritage places can be tangible physical places or conceptual spaces, or both. Practically speaking, they are almost certainly both because a tangible place that has lost its conceptual space and meaning is not likely to survive. Caretaking will only continue as long as there is some associated meaning (even if only for some very small and dedicated group). We illustrate our model in figure 11.1.

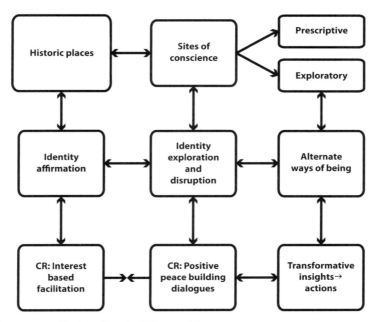

Figure 11.1   Heritage Peacebuilding model.

The three spaces across the top represent heritage places. The first box, representing historic sites in general, connects with identity affirmation in the way Rounds refers to it (see chapter 10). The second box represents those heritage places or place-based projects that have taken on the work of sites of conscience, whether or not they have formally joined the International Coalition of Sites of Conscience. It is only slightly smaller than the first box because we believe that most historic sites could become sites of conscience, since history is replete with opportunities to examine the roots of current social issues. In many ways, certain individual projects—whether service learning, research focused, or compliance driven—could be considered conceptually as sites of conscience.

The third box in the top row represents two types of sites of conscience that we have observed. The prescriptive type approaches connections between past and present in an authoritarian way, directing and even demanding visitors to think in a certain way. This kind of approach is not all that different from that taken at many historic places that are not consciously or intentionally sites of conscience; both are relying on a commitment to some embedded and always imperfectly perceived truth. The exploratory type approaches connections between past and present as relationships that visitors need to work through for themselves, in concert with their own sets of values, even as those values may be deeply challenged by engaging with issues that are raised or nurtured at an intentional site of conscience.

Moving from the top row in our model clockwise to the second row, we believe that the prescriptive type is less likely to invite the contemplation and disruptive moments that may spark an interest in alternative ways of being. Instead, visitors are more likely to be affirmed in their beliefs and values, whether they are echoed in the heritage displays or different enough to arouse anger and suspicion. The exploratory approach requires a courageous acceptance of the process of coming to public judgment, even while committed to a particular ethical stance about the meaning and usefulness of heritage for contemporary social justice.

The horizontal middle row concerns identity work as it connects to different intentions of the heritage places. Identity exploration and disruption occupies the center space, interconnecting positively or negatively with identity affirmation as provoked by intentional sites of conscience. This central idea of disruption can lead to ideas about alternative ways of being as consciousness is raised about past and present issues. Thinking about and trying out alternative ways of being, often through genuine human empathy, can be truly transformative. There are transformative moments that come from insights: both the "ah-ha" moment of clarity, which may be experienced as a flash of positive insight, and the "uh-oh" moment, in which one recognizes—perhaps also in a flash—that one has been quite wrong and must search for a new way of being or a new value system.

The bottom row of the model shows the opposing categories of conflict resolution (CR) and possible outcomes of alternative CR applied within heritage places. For example, the column on the left includes heritage places of all types that serve a variety of purposes. They are places for identity work and affirmation and serve to maintain the status quo. They are underlain by the same social metaphors that support interest-based CR rooted in Western economic relationships of the buyer-seller model. These heritage places perpetuate and support these deeply embedded social relationships.

We see great promise in the dynamic represented in the right-hand two-thirds of our model. We envision positive peacebuilding dialogues as an approach to conflict resolution, especially when the conflict is long lasting and maintained by structural violence and cultural violence. Sites of conscience, whether in the formal Coalition network or acting with the same intention through a specific heritage project or as service learning in higher education, act to raise consciousness. Civic engagement practitioners provide the tools of dialogue and mediation skills to engage and empower people to work through issues in the public sphere, including those involving any counterpublics, and come to the kind of high quality public judgment necessary for a democracy to flourish.

What Is Next?

The ways that heritage workers conceptualize and practice their work are changing. Our work is applied anthropology and our intention for this book is to provoke heritage work that is intentional about building peace and social justice.

How would you do the work of the sites of conscience in your own communities? How do we turn our historic places into sites of conscience, into powerful historic places for dialogue about pressing issues? There are innumerable approaches that might be undertaken by archaeologists, museum practitioners, and other heritage workers to use our expertise and our knowledge base to work toward the public good.

We believe one very good place to start is the tactical notebook entitled, "The Power of Place: how historic sites can engage citizens in human rights issues" published by the New Tactics Project of the Center for Victims of Torture (Ševčenko 2004). That notebook includes several case studies from founding sites in the International Coalition of Sites of Conscience, followed by specific steps for transferring the tactics used to other historic sites or museums to create a space for dialogue about pressing issues. Such transformational opportunities can be nurtured in our own communities. We have included these steps below in table 11.1. This is an easy place to start and we recommend consulting the full notebook.

Freedom, justice, and rights are a few of the sturdy threads that run through this book. Recall the two examples in the introduction: Gable's suggestion that we examine the nature of privilege at our "inadvertent white identity shrines" and open up different conversations; and Weik's challenge to enable people to have empowering conversations about freedom and struggle. We started there to illustrate the power of the heritage arena in defining, challenging, and rethinking the structural narratives of our democracy.

TABLE 11.1   THE POWER OF PLACE: HOW HISTORIC SITES CAN ENGAGE CITIZENS IN HUMAN RIGHTS
ISSUES. USED WITH PERMISSION OF THE CENTER FOR VICTIMS OF TORTURE. WWW.CVT.ORG.

Transferring the tactic

Whether you are a small grassroots victims' group or an established human rights organization, whether you have a traditional museum or no museum at all, if you seek to harness the power of places of memory to inspire dialogue and citizen action, keep the following in mind:

Use the power of place. Connect visitors to the specific history of your site; understand and use the ways the spaces make people feel to help them connect to the broader issues you are trying to raise.

Make the process part of the product. Controversy is too often avoided as something damaging to an institution or a project; in fact, engaging conflicting perspectives is one of the greatest opportunities for sites of conscience. Involve stakeholders from different perspectives in the development of the project. The process of developing the story and experience is a productive starting point for dialogue about the contemporary issues at stake. Involving different perspectives at the outset ensures that these perspectives will be raised in the exhibit and that different groups will participate in dialogues after the project is completed.

Develop different forms of dialogue that can engage people with different amounts of time to spend, different cultural backgrounds, different personalities, etc. In addition to offering an in-depth dialogue program after the tours, sites are developing ways to generate discussions among visitors during the tours. Others are also developing other ways to stimulate dialogue and address contemporary issues through the web, printed material and other media.

Manage visitor expectations. To prepare visitors for the sensitive issues they may encounter, sites work to communicate their commitment to addressing contemporary questions through information on web sites, at visitors centers, by distributing maps of the site that indicate where visitors will encounter material on the present day and by training front-line staff to speak to visitors before they go on the tour.

Serve as an open forum. Raising both sides of an issue and encouraging debate stimulates citizen participation more effectively than teaching a single story to a passive audience. But museums must find ways to do this without becoming moral relativists or appearing to excuse or condone perpetrators.

Serve as an ongoing forum. Memorials must be active places where issues are constantly debated, where stories are told and retold. The site and program must be flexible enough to accommodate the ways the meaning of the past changes for each generation, to be constantly reinvented. A static narrative or permanent sculpture will foreclose dialogue and become obsolete in short order.

Focus on individual human experience as a starting point. This helps visitors to connect the story to their own personal experiences and imagine what they would have done in each situation. This kind of imagining is the first step in inspiring people to take action.

TABLE 11.1   THE POWER OF PLACE: HOW HISTORIC SITES CAN ENGAGE CITIZENS IN HUMAN RIGHTS ISSUES. USED WITH PERMISSION OF THE CENTER FOR VICTIMS OF TORTURE. WWW.CVT.ORG. (CONTINUED)

Where To Begin?

Groups that are exploring how a place of memory could help address a human rights issue in their communities might begin by bringing key constituencies together for a discussion of the following questions:

1. Identify a place associated with the history of a conflict that is still unresolved today. (This place could be somewhere a human rights abuse occurred, a human rights victory occurred, or an issue of rights was debated. It could be a place that already has a museum or a memorial or a place that does not.) What happened there?

2. What do you think people would feel or learn by visiting this place? What perspectives would it give them on the current conflict?

3. Imagine using this place to negotiate a conflict. What individuals or groups would you bring to this place? What would they see and do there? What questions would you discuss with them?

4. How would you present the story of what happened at this place—what would people see and do there?

5. How would you commemorate what happened in a way that allows for ongoing dialogue and future reinterpretation?

6. What questions would you discuss with people here? How would you engage them in dialogue around these questions?

7. What difference would it make to have this dialogue at this place? How do you think remembering the history of this place could help to negotiate the current conflict?

8. What challenges do you think you would face in developing this place as a center to address contemporary issues and to engage people in dialogue? How would you overcome these challenges?

9. What is the potential impact of using this place as a center for ongoing dialogue on human rights issues? How can the experience of visiting this place help promote peace and negotiate the current conflict in a way other strategies cannot? In other words, what difference does it make?

We organized this book as a layered and cumulative sharing of stories and we hope that the storytelling does not end here. Our stories about the past weigh on the present and have implications for the ways we choose to shape tomorrow. We have called for an intentional reframing of our heritage disciplines to start in the public sphere and to participate in public problem solving as if our lives depended on it.

References

Adams, E. Charles. 1984. Archaeology and the Native American: A Case at Hopi. In *Ethics and Values in Archaeology*, ed. Ernestene L. Green, 236–263. New York: Free Press.

Ali, Saleem H. 2007. Introduction: A Natural Connection between Ecology and Peace. In *Peace Parks: Conservation and Conflict Resolution,* ed. Saleem H. Ali, 1–18. Cambridge, MA: MIT Press.

———. 2010. Can An Ecological Peace Park Catalyze Peace Between Syria and Israel? *Green Prophet.* http://www.greenprophet.com/2010/01/syria-israel-peace-park/ (accessed May 13, 2011).

Alinsky, Saul D. 1945. *Reveille for Radicals.* Chicago: University of Chicago Press.

American Association of Museums. 2002. *Mastering Civic Engagement: A Challenge to Museums.* Washington, DC: American Association of Museums.

Anawak, Jack. 1989. Inuit Perceptions of the Past. In *Who Needs the Past?: Indigenous Values and Archaeology*, ed. Robert Layton, 45–50. London: Unwin Hyman.

Anico, Marta, and Elsa Peralta. 2009. Introduction. In *Heritage and Identity: Engagement and Demission in the Contemporary World*, ed. Marta Anico and Elsa Peralta, 1–11. New York: Routledge.

Arizpe, Lourdes. 2000. Cultural Heritage and Globalization. In *Values and Heritage Conservation, Research Report,* ed. Erica Avrami, Randall Mason, and Marta de la Torre. 32–37. Los Angeles: Getty Conservation Institute.

Association of American Colleges and Universities. 2010. *Civic Engagement.* Association of American Colleges & Universities. http://www.aacu.org/resources/civicengagement/index.cfm (accessed July 1, 2010).

Atalay, Sonya. 2006. Indigenous Archaeology as Decolonizing Practice. *American Indian Quarterly* 30 (3/4): 280–310.

Avrami, Erica, Randall Mason, and Marta de la Torre. 2000. *Values and Heritage Conservation, Research Report.* Los Angeles: Getty Conservation Institute.

Avruch, Kevin. 2012. *Context and Pretext in Conflict Resolution: Culture, Identity, Power and Practice.* Boulder, CO: Paradigm.

Bales, Kevin. 2004. *Disposable People: New Slavery in the Global Economy.* Berkeley and Los Angeles: University of California Press.

———. 2005. *Understanding Global Slavery: A Reader.* Berkeley and Los Angeles: University of California Press.

Baram, Uzi. 2009. Learning Service and Civic Engagement: A Historic Cemetery as a Site for Grappling with Community, Politics, and Commemoration. In Nassaney and Levine 2009, 110–121.

Battle-Baptiste, Whitney. 2011. *Black Feminist Archaeology.* Walnut Creek, CA: Left Coast Press.

Beik, Mildred Allen. 2002. The Significance of the Lattimer Massacre: Who Owns History? *Pennsylvania History,* 69 (1): 58–70.

Berube, Maurice R., and Clair T. Berube. 2010. *The Moral University.* Lanham, MD: Rowman and Littlefield.

Blakey, Michael. 1987. Intrinsic Social and Political Bias in the History of American Physical Anthropology: With Special Reference to the Work of Aleš Hrdlička. *Critique of Anthropology* 7 (2): 7–35.

Boas, Franz. 1911. *The Mind of Primitive Man.* Boston, MA: Macmillan, Co.

———. 1912. *Changes in Bodily Form of Descendants of Immigrants.* New York: Columbia University Press.

Bohannon, John. 2008. Team Unveils Mideast Peace Plan. *Science* 320 (5874): 302.

Bok, Derek. 1982. *Higher Learning.* Cambridge, MA: Harvard University.

Bonacich, Edna, and Richard P. Appelbaum. 2000. *Behind the Label: Inequality in the Los Angeles Apparel Industry.* Berkeley and Los Angeles: University of California Press.

Boulding, Kenneth E. 1978. *Stable Peace.* Austin: University of Texas Press.

Bourdieu. Pierre. 1977. *Outline of a Theory of Practice.* Cambridge: Cambridge University Press. (Orig. pub. 1972.)

Bowles, Samuel, and Herbert Gintis. 2002. Social Capital and Community Governance. *The Economic Journal* 112 (483): F419–436.

Bowley, Graham. 2010. The Academic-Industrial Complex. *New York Times Sunday Business,* August 1, 2010, 1, 4.

Brandon, Jamie C., and James M. Davidson. 2005. The Landscape of Van Winkle's Mill: Identity, Myth, and Modernity in the Ozark Upland South. *Historical Archaeology* 39 (3): 113–131.

Brooks, Ethel C. 2007. *Unraveling the Garment Industry: Transnational Organizing and Women's Work.* Minneapolis: University of Minnesota Press.

Bruner, M. Lane. 2010. The Public Work of Critical Political Communication. In *The Public Work of Rhetoric: Citizen-Scholars and Civic Engagement,* ed. John M. Ackerman, and David J. Coogan, 56–75. Columbia: University of South Carolina Press.

Campus Compact. 2013. Campus Compact: Educating Citizens, Building Communities. (a) Who We Are, http://www.compact.org/about/history-mission-vision/; (b) Presidents' Resources, Presidents' statement of principles, http://www.compact.

org/resources-for-presidents/presidents-statement-of-principles/; (c) Presidents'
Resources, Presidents' Declaration on the Civic Responsibility of Higher Education, http://www.compact.org/resources-for-presidents/presidents-declaration-
on-the-civic-responsibility-of-higher-education/ and http://www.compact.org/
wp-content/uploads/2009/02/Presidents-Declaration.pdf; (d) Initiatives, The Research University Civic Engagement Network (TRUCEN), http://www.compact.
org/initiatives/trucen/ and http://www.compact.org/wp-content/uploads/2013/04/
TRUCEN-Mission-Visions-Goals-5-11-10.pdf (accessed Nov. 26, 2013).

Carcamo, Cindy. 2013. Judge Upholds Arizona Law Banning Ethnic Studies Classes.
Los Angeles Times, March 12, 2013. http://www.latimes.com/news/nation/nation-
now/la-na-nn-ff-ethnic-studies-arizona-20130312,0,6256895.story (accessed May
8, 2013).

Champion, Erik. 2011. *Playing with the Past*. London: Springer-Verlag.

Checker, Melissa. 2002. 'It's in the Air': Redefining the Environment as a New Metaphor for Old Social Justice Struggles. *Human Organization* 61 (1): 94–105.

Chollett, Donna L. 1999. Global Competition and Community: The Struggle for
Social Justice. *Research in Economic Anthropology* 20:19-47.

Christian, Marcus B. 1972 *Negro Ironworkers in Louisiana, 1718–1900*. Gretna, LA:
Pelican.

Chronicle of Higher Education. 2003. China and a New Space Race; Modern Slavery;
Crackdown in Cuba. *Chronicle of Higher Education* 50 (5): B6.

Clark, Kate. 2005. The Bigger Picture: Archaeology and Values in Long-term Cultural
Resource Management. In *Heritage of Value, Archaeology of Renown; Reshaping
Archaeological Assessment and Significance*, ed. Clay Mathers, Timothy Darvill,
and Barbara J. Little, 317–330. Gainesville: University Press of Florida.

Coalition for Civic Engagement and Leadership, Steering Committee of. 2005. Working Definition of Civic Engagement. http://web.archive.org/web/20100529194548/
http://www.terpimpact.umd.edu/content2.asp?cid=7&sid=41 (accessed August
10, 2013).

Colwell-Chanthaphonh, Chip, and T. J. Ferguson. 2004. Virtue Ethics and the Practice of History: Native Americans and Archaeologists Along the San Pedro Valley
of Arizona. *Journal of Social Archaeology* 4 (1): 5–27.

———, eds. 2008. *Collaboration in Archaeological Practice: Engaging Descendant
Communities*. Lanham, MD: AltaMira Press.

———. 2008. Introduction: The Collaborative Continuum. In Colwell-Chanthaphonh and Ferguson 2008, 1–32.

Creative News Group, WNET. 2013. "Banned in Arizona." *Need to Know*. February
15, 2013. http://www.pbs.org/wnet/need-to-know/video/need-to-know-febru-
ary-15-2013/16294/ (accessed November 25, 2013).

Crowley, Jocelyn Elise, and Theda Skocpol. 2001. The Rush to Organize: Explaining
Associational Formation in the United States, 1860s–1920s. *American Journal of
Political Science* 45 (4): 813–829.

Cruz Cuison, Rose. 2000. The Construction of Labor Abuse in the Mariana Islands as
Anti-American. *UCLA Asian Pacific American Law Journal* 6:61–85.

Davis, James E. 1998. *Frontier Illinois*. Bloomington: Indiana University Press.

de la Torre, Ferdie. 2007. Dotts: It's the End for All CNMI Garment Factories. *Saipan Tribune.com*, May 30, 2007. http://www.saipantribune.com/newsstory. aspx?cat=1&newsID=68959 (accessed September 5, 2012).

de la Torre, Marta, ed. 2002. *Assessing the Values of Cultural Heritage*. Los Angeles: Getty Conservation Institute.

Democratic Underground. 2013. FDR's Unfinished "Second Bill of Rights"—and Why We Need it Now. http://www.democraticunderground.com/discuss/duboard. php?az=view_all&address=364x2848856 (accessed August 6, 2013).

Dew, Charles B. 1966. *Ironmaker to the Confederacy: Joseph R. Anderson and the Tredegar Iron Works*. New Haven, CT: Yale University Press.

———. 1994a *Bonds of Iron: Master and Slave at Buffalo Forge*. New York: W. W. Norton.

———. 1994b David Ross and the Oxford Iron Works: A Study of Industrial Slavery in the Early Nineteenth-Century South. *William and Mary Quarterly* 31 (2): 189–224.

De Wet, Phillip. 2012. Marikana: How the Wage War Was Won. *Mail and Guardian*, September 21, 2012. http://mg.co.za/article/2012-09-21-00-marikana-how-the-wage-war-was-won (accessed January 16, 2013).

Dodson, Michael. 1993. First Report 1993, Aboriginal and Torres Islander Social Justice Commission. http://www.austlii.edu.au/au/other/IndigLRes/1993/3/index. html (accessed Nov. 25, 2013).

Doyle, Debbie Ann. 2012. The Future of Local Historical Societies. *Perspectives Online* 50:9. http://www.historians.org/perspectives/issues/2012/1212/Future-of-Local-Historical-Societies.cfm (accessed August 12, 2012).

Echo-Hawk, Roger C. 2000 Ancient History in the New World: Integrating Oral Traditions and the Archaeological Record. *American Antiquity* 65 (2): 267–290.

Ehrlich, Thomas. 2000a. Civic Engagement. Measuring Up 2000: The State-by-State Report Card for Higher Education. http://web.archive.org/web/20061202110958/ http://measuringup.highereducation.org/2000/articles/ThomasEhrlich.cfm (accessed November 25, 2013).

———, ed. 2000b. *Civic Responsibility and Higher Education*. Phoenix, AZ: Oryx Press.

———. 2000c. Preface. In Ehrlich 2000a, iii–x.

Eyler, Janet, and Dwight E. Giles, Jr. 1999. *Where's the Learning in Service-Learning?* San Francisco: Jossey-Bass.

Farrell, Betty, and Maria Medvedeva. 2010. *Demographic Transformation and the Future of Museums*. Washington, DC: American Association of Museums,

Farrow, Anne, Joel Long, and Jenifer Frank. 2005. *Complicity: How the North Promoted, Prolonged, and Profited from Slavery*. New York: Ballantine Books.

Faust, Drew Gilpin. 2009. The University's Crisis of Purpose. Crossroads essay series. *New York Times*, September 1, 2009. http://www.nytimes.com/2009/09/06/books/ review/Faust-t.html?pagewanted=all&_r=0.

Fennell, Christopher. 2010. Damaging Detours: Routes, Racism, and New Philadelphia. *Historical Archaeology* 44 (1): 138–154.

Fennell, Christopher C., Terrance J. Martin, and Paul A. Shackel, eds. 2010. New Philadelphia: Race, Community, and the Illinois Frontier. *Historical Archaeology*, 44 (1).

Ferguson, T. J. 1984. Archaeological Ethics and Values in a Tribal Cultural Resource Management Program at the Pueblo of Zuni. In *Ethics and Values in Archaeology*, ed. Ernestene L. Green, 224–235. New York: Free Press.

———. 1996 Native Americans and the Practice of Archaeology. *Annual Review of Anthropology* 25:63-79.

Ferragina, Emanuele. 2010. Social Capital and Equality: Tocqueville's Legacy; Rethinking Social Capital in Relation with Income Inequalities. *The Tocqueville Review* 31 (1): 73–98.

Fine, Ben. 2001. *Social Capital versus Social Theory: Political Economy and Social Science at the Turn of the Millennium*. London: Routledge.

Fisher, Roger, William Ury, and Bruce Patton. 2011. *Getting to Yes: Negotiating Agreement Without Giving In*. New York: Penguin.

Ford, Anabel. 2011. Afterword, El Pilar and Maya Cultural Heritage: Reflections of a Cheerful Pessimist. In *Contested Cultural Heritage: Religion, Nationalism, Erasure, and Exclusion in a Global World*, ed. Helaine Silverman, 261–265. New York: Springer.

Francioni, Francesco. 2008. Culture, Heritage and Human Rights: An Introduction. In *Cultural Human Rights*, ed. Francesco Francioni, and Martin Scheinin, 1–15. Leiden, Netherlands: Martinus Nijhoff.

Gable, Eric. 2009. Labor and Leisure at Monticello: Or Representing Race Instead of Class at an Inadvertent White Identity Shrine. In Anico and Peralta 2009, 143–155.

Galtung, Johan. 1969. Violence, Peace, and Peace Research. *Journal of Peace Research* 6 (3): 167–191.

———. 1990. Cultural Violence. *Journal of Peace Research* 27 (3): 291–305.

Ganz, Marshall. 2011. Public Narrative, Collective Action, and Power. In *Accountability Through Public Opinion From Inertia to Public Action*, ed. Sina Odugbemi and Taeku Lee, 273–289. Washington, DC: World Bank.

Gates, Christopher T. 2002. The Civic Landscape. In American Association of Museums 2002, 23–28.

Giroux, Henry A. 2007. *The University in Chains: Confronting the Military-Industrial-Academic Complex*. Boulder, CO: Paradigm.

Glover, Nikolas. 2008. Co-produced Histories: Mapping the Uses and Narratives of History in the Tourist Age. *The Public Historian* 30 (1): 105–124.

Gwaltney, Thomas. 2004. *New Philadelphia Project Pedestrian Survey: Final Report and Catalog. Phase I Archeology at the Historic Town of New Philadelphia, Illinois*. Bethesda, MD: ArGIS Consultants. http://www.heritage.umd.edu/CHRSWeb/New%20Philadelphia/NP_Final_Report_View.pdf (accessed December 15, 2011).

Handsman, Russell G., and Trudie Lamb Richmond. 1995. Confronting Colonialism: The Mahican and Schaghticoke Peoples and Us. In *Making Alternative Histories: The Practice of Archaeology and History in Non-Western Settings*, ed. Peter R. Schmidt and Thomas C. Patterson, 87–117. Santa Fe, NM: School of American Research.

Hanifan, Lyda J. 1916. The Rural School Community Centre. *Annals of the American Academy of Political and Social Sciences* 67:130–38.

Hobsbawm, Eric. 1993. The New Threat to History, *New York Review of Books*, December16, 1993, 62–64.

Holder, Cindy. 2008. Culture as an Activity and a Human Right: An Important Advance for Indigenous Peoples and International Law. *Alternatives: Global, Local, Political* 33 (1): 7–28.

Horwitz, Tony. 2008. *A Voyage Long and Strange: On the trail of Vikings, Conquistadors, Lost Colonists, and other Adventurers in Early America*. New York: Picador.

Howard, Peter. 2003. *Heritage: Management, Interpretation, Identity*. London: Continuum.

International Coalition of Sites of Conscience. 2012. International Coalition of Sites of Conscience. http://www.sitesofconscience.org (accessed August 20, 2012).

Isaacs, Harold R. 1975. *Idols of the Tribe: Group Identity and Political Change*. New York: Harper and Row.

Jacoby, Barbara. 1996. *Service Learning in Higher Education*. San Francisco: Jossey-Bass.

Jensen, Uffe Juul. 2000. Cultural Heritage, Liberal Education, and Human Flourishing. In Avrami, Mason, and de la Torre 2000, 38–43.

Johnston, Barbara Rose, ed. 2011. *Life and Death Matters: Human Rights, Environment, and Social Justice*. Walnut Creek, CA: Left Coast Press.

———. 2011. Human Rights, Environmental Quality, and Social Justice. In *Life and Death Matters: Human Rights, Environment, and Social Justice*, ed. Barbara Rose Johnston, 9–27. Walnut Creek, CA: Left Coast Press.

Kendall, J. C. 1990. *Combining Service and Learning: A Resource Book for Community and Public Service*. Raleigh, NC: National Society for Experiential Education.

Kerber, Jordan. 2006. *Cross-Cultural Collaboration: Native Peoples and Archaeology in the Northeastern United States*. Lincoln: University of Nebraska Press.

Khadaroo, Stacy Teicher. 2010. After Immigration Crackdown, Arizona Targets Ethnic Studies. *Christian Science Monitor*, May 13, 2010. http://www.csmonitor.com/USA/Education/2010/0513/After-immigration-crackdown-Arizona-targets-ethnic-studies?nav=328007-csm_article-bottomRelated (accessed August 12, 2012).

King, Charlotte. 2007. *New Philadelphia: A Multiracial Town on the Illinois Frontier. Teaching with Historic Places Lesson Plans*. Washington DC: National Park Service.

Kloppenberg, James T. 2006. Franklin Delano Roosevelt, Visionary. *Reviews in American History* 34 (4): 509–520.

Laing, Aislinn. 2012. Striking South African Miners "Were Shot in the Back." *Telegraph*, August 27, 2012. http://www.telegraph.co.uk/news/worldnews/africaandindianocean/southafrica/9501910/Striking-South-African-miners-were-shot-in-the-back.html (accessed August 10, 2013).

Lakeland. 2013. Lakeland History. http://lakelandchp.com/history (accessed March 22, 2013).

Lakeland Community Heritage Project. 2009. *Lakeland: African Americans in College Park.* Charleston, SC: Arcadia.

Langfield, Michele, William Logan, and Mairead Nic Craith, eds. 2010. *Cultural Diversity, Heritage and Human Rights: Intersections in Theory and Practice.* London: Routledge.

Lempert, D. H. 1995. *Escape from the Ivory Tower: Student Adventures in Democratic Experiential Learning Education.* San Francisco: Jossey-Bass.

Lewis, Ronald L. 1979. *Coal, Iron, and Slaves: Industrial Slavery in Maryland and Virginia.* Westport, CT: Greenwood.

Liebhold, Peter, and Harry R. Rubenstein. 2003. Bringing Sweatshops into the Museum. In *Sweatshop USA: The American Sweatshop in Historical and Global Perspective,* ed. Daniel Bender and Richard Greenwald, 57–73. New York: Routledge.

Lippert, Dorothy. 2008. Not the End, Not the Middle, But the Beginning: Repatriation as a Transformative Mechanism for Archaeologists and Indigenous Peoples. In Colwell-Chanthaphonh and Ferguson 2008, 119–130.

Little, Barbara J., ed. 2002. *Public Benefits of Archaeology.* Gainesville: University Press of Florida.

———. 2007 *Historical Archaeology: Why the Past Matters.* Walnut Creek, CA: Left Coast Press.

———. 2009. Forum: What Can Archaeology Do for Justice, Peace, Community and the Earth? *Historical Archaeology* 43 (4): 115–119.

———. 2010. Epilogue: Changing the World with Archaeology: Archaeology Activism. In *Archaeologists as Activists: Can Archaeologists Change the World?,* ed. Jay Stottman, 154–158. Tuscaloosa: University of Alabama Press.

———. 2011. Heritage, Resilience, and Peace. *Heritage & Society* 4 (2): 187–198.

———. 2012. Envisioning engaged and useful archaeologies. In *Archaeology in Society: its relevance in the modern world,* ed. Marcy Rockman, and Joseph Flatman, 277–289. New York: Springer.

———. 2013. Archaeology and place-based heritage for transformational conflict resolution and peace building. Paper presented at the 2013 Annual Meeting of the Northeastern Anthropological Association, College Park, Maryland.

Little, Barbara J., and Larry J. Zimmerman. 2010. In the Public Interest: Creating a More Activist, Civically-Engaged Archaeology. In *Voices in American Archaeology,* ed. Wendy Ashmore, Dorothy Lippert, and Barbara Mills, 131–159. Washington, DC: Society for American Archaeology.

Little, Barbara J., and Paul A. Shackel, eds. 2007. *Archaeology as a Tool of Civic Engagement.* Lanham, MD: AltaMira Press.

Loewen, James. 2005. *Sundowner Towns: A Hidden Dimension of American Racism.* New York: New Press.

Logan, William. 2012. Cultural Diversity, Cultural Heritage and Human Rights: Towards Heritage Management as Human Rights-based Cultural Practice. *International Journal of Heritage Studies* 18 (3): 231–244.

Logan, William, Michele Langfield, and Mairead Nic Craith. 2010. Intersecting concepts and Practices. In Langfield, Logan, and Craith 2010, 3–20.

Louie, Miriam Ching Yoon. 2001. *Sweatshop Warriors: Immigrant Women Workers Take on the Global Factory*. Cambridge, MA: South End Press.

MacDonald, Sharon. 2009. Unsettling Memories: Intervention and Controversy Over Difficult Public Heritage. In Anico and Peralta 2009, 93–104.

Mandela, Nelson. 2011. Peace Park Foundation. http://www.peaceparks.org/ (accessed May 13, 2011).

Markkula Center for Applied Ethics. 2013. Ethical Decision Making. Santa Clara University. http://www.scu.edu/ethics/practicing/decision/ (accessed June 30, 2013).

Marris, Emma. 2011. *Rambunctious Garden: Saving Nature in a Post-Wild World*. New York: Bloomsbury.

Mason, Ronald J. 2000. Archaeology and Native American Oral Traditions. *American Antiquity* 65 (2): 239–266.

McEwen, Marylu K. 1996. New Perspectives on Identity Development. In *Student Services: A Handbook for the Profession*, ed. S. R. Komives, D. B. Woodward, Jr., and Associates, 188–217. San Francisco: Jossey-Bass.

McGuire, Randall H. 1997. Why Have Archaeologists Thought the Real Indians Were Dead and What Can We Do About it? In *Indians & Anthropologists: Vine Deloria Jr., and the Critique of Anthropology*, ed. Thomas Biolsi, and Larry J. Zimmerman, 63–91. Tucson: University of Arizona Press.

McGurrin, Danielle. 2007. Fabrication: Corporate and Governmental Crime in the Apparel Industry. PhD diss., University of South Florida.

Meyer-Bisch, Patrice. 2013. Defining cultural rights. *Compendium of Cultural Policies and Trends in Europe*, 14th ed. Council of Europe/ERICarts. http://www.cultural-policies.net/web/compendium-topics.php?aid=171 (accessed March 31, 2013).

Minteer, Ben A., and Stephen J. Pyne. 2012. Restoring the Narrative of American Environmentalism. *Restoration Ecology* 21 (1): 6–11.

Misulich, Robert J. 2011. A Lesser-Known Immigration Crisis: Federal Immigration Law in the Commonwealth of the Northern Mariana Islands. *Pacific Rim Law & Policy Journal* 20 (1): 211–235.

Moyer, Teresa S. 2004. "To Have and Enjoy the Liberty of Conscience" Community-Responsive Museum Outreach Education at the Bowne House. In *Places in Mind: Public Archaeology as Applied Anthropology*, ed. Paul A. Shackel, and Erve J. Chambers, 85–100. New York: Routledge.

Mukhopadhyay, Carol C., and Yolanda T. Moses. 1997. Re-establishing "Race" in Anthropological Discourse. *American Anthropologist* 99 (3): 517–533.

Musil, Caryn McTighe. 2003. Educating for Citizenship. *Peer Review* 5 (3): 4–8.

Nas, P. J. M. 1994. Social Justice in the Third World City: An Essay on Urban Poverty. *International Journal of Anthropology* 9 (1): 35–40.

Nassaney, Michael S. 2009. The Reform of Archaeological Pedagogy and Practice through Community Service Learning. In Nassaney and Levine 2009, 3–35.

Nassaney, Michael S., and Mary Ann Levine, eds. 2009. *Archaeology and Community Service Learning.* Gainesville: University Press of Florida.

National Geographic. 2011. Promote International Cooperation and Conservation through Peace Parks. *Global Action Atlas.* http://www.actionatlas.org/conservation/migrations/jordan-river-peace-park/summary/pa3458122DE03667DC6F (accessed May 13, 2011).

National Museum of American History. 1998. *Between a Rock and a Hard Place: A History of American Sweatshops, 1820–present.* National Museum of American History, Smithsonian Institution, Washington, DC. http://www.americanhistory.si.edu/sweatshops/ (accessed September 13, 2012).

Nelson, Robert S., and Margaret Olin, eds. 2003. *Monuments and Memory, Made and Unmade.* Chicago: University Press of Chicago.

———. 2003. Introduction. In Nelson and Olin 2003, 1–10.

Nicholas, George P., John R. Welch, and Eldon C. Yellowhorn. 2008. Collaborative Encounters. In Colwell-Chanthaphonh and Ferguson 2008, 273–298..

Nilsson, Magnus. 2011. Swedish Working Class Literature and the Class Politics of Heritage. In *Heritage, Labour and the Working Class*, ed. Laurajane Smith, Paul A. Shackel, and Gary Campbell, 178–191. New York: Routledge.

Novak, Michael. 1978. *The Guns of Lattimer.* New Brunswick, NJ: Transaction Publishers.

———. 2000. Defining Social Justice. *First Things: A Monthly Journal of Religion and Public Life.* (December): 11–13. http://www.firstthings.com/article/2007/01/defining-social-justice-29 (accessed August 10, 2012).

Oliver-Smith, Anthony. 2006. Communities after Catastrophe: Reconstructing the Material, Reconstituting the Social. In *Community Building in the Twenty-First Century*, ed. Stanley E. Hyland, 45–70. Santa Fe, NM: School of American Research.

Parker, Patricia L., and Thomas F. King. 1998. National Register of Historic Places Guidelines for Evaluating and Documenting Traditional Cultural Properties. http://www.nps.gov/history/nr/publications/bulletins/nrb38/ (accessed August 18, 2013).

Pastore, E. 2009. *The Future of Museums and Libraries: A Discussion Guide.* IMLS-2009-RES-02. Washington, DC: Institute of Museum and Library Services>

Peace Park Foundation (PPF). 2011. Origins. Peace Park Foundation. www.peaceparks.org/ (accessed May 13, 2011).

Putnam, Robert D. 2000. *Bowling Alone: The Collapse and Revival of American Community.* New York: Simon and Schuster.

Pyburn, K. Anne, and Richard Wilk. 1995. Responsible Archaeology is Applied Anthropology. In *Ethics in American Archaeology*, ed. Mark Lynott, and Alison Wylie, 71–76. Washington, DC: Society for American Archaeology.

Rabinow, Paul. 1992. For Hire: Resolutely Late Modern. In *Recapturing Anthropology*, ed. Richard Fox, 59–72. Santa Fe, NM: School of American Research.

Ramaley, Judith, Joan Ferrini-Mundy, Paul Targonski, Frances Lawrenz. 2009. Meeting the Standards of Scientific Inquiry in Community-Engaged Research. Symposium at University of Minnesota, March 10, 2009. http://engagement.umn.edu/symposia (accessed August 12, 2012).

Roseberry, William. 1992. Multiculturalism and the Challenge of Anthropology. *Social Research* 59 (4): 841–858.

Rosen, Ellen Israel. 2002. *Making Sweatshops: The Globalization of the U.S. Apparel Industry.* Berkeley and Los Angeles: University of California Press.

Rosenberger, Nancy R. 1999. Global Capital in Small Town USA: Justice Versus Efficiency for Bus Drivers. *Urban Anthropology* 28 (3–4): 447–81.

Rosenblatt, Gideon. 2010. The Engagement Pyramid: Six Levels of Connecting People and Social Change. Idealware. http://www.idealware.org/articles/engagement-pyramid-six-levels-connecting-people-and-social-change (accessed August 10, 2012).

Roosevelt, Franklin Delano. 1944. State of the Union Message to Congress, January 11, 1944. http://www.presidency.ucsb.edu/ws/index.php?pid=16518 (accessed November 25, 2013).

Ross, Robert J. R. 2004. *Slaves to Fashion: Poverty and Abuse in the New Sweatshops.* Ann Arbor: University of Michigan Press.

Rounds, Jay. 2006. Doing Identity Work in Museums. *Curator* 49:2:133–150.

Russell, Molly. 2011. Principles of Successful Civic Engagement in the National Park Service. Washington DC: National Park Service. http://www.nps.gov/civic/resources/CE%20study07.pdf (accessed August 16, 2012).

Russell-Ciardi, Maggie. 2008. The Museum as a Democracy-Building Institution: Reflections on the Shared Journeys Program at the Lower East Side Tenement Museum. *Public Historian* 30 (1): 39–52.

Saguaro Seminar. 2000. BetterTogether. http://www.bettertogether.org/pdfs/FullReportText.pdf (accessed August 10, 2013).

Saunders. 1999. Sweatshops Aren't History: Museum traces resurgence of sweatshops in exhibit apparel industry tried to stop. *New York Teacher.* www.newyorkteacher.org (accessed July 6, 2005).

Scham, Sandra A., and Adel Yahya. 2003. Heritage and Reconciliation. *Journal of Social Archaeology* 3 (3): 399–416.

Ševčenko, Liz. 2004. *The Power of Place: how historic sites can engage citizens in human rights issues.* A Tactical Notebook published by the New Tactics Project of the Center for Victims of Torture. http://www.newtactics.org/sites/default/files/resources/Power-Place-EN.pdf (accessed August 12, 2012).

Ševčenko, Liz, and Maggie Russell-Ciardi. 2008. Forward to "Sites of Conscience: Opening Historic Sites for Civic Dialogue." *Public Historian* 30 (1): 9–15.

Shackel, Paul A. 2005. Local Identity, National Memory and Heritage Tourism: Creating a Sense of Place With Archaeology. *SAA Archaeological Record* 5 (3): 33–35.

———. 2007. Civic Engagement and Social Justice: Addressing Race and Labor Issues. In Little and Shackel 2007, 243–262.

———. 2009. Engaging Communities in the Heartland: An Archaeology of a Multiracial Community. *Practicing Anthropology* 31 (3): 11–14.

———. 2009b. *The Archaeology of American Labor and Working Class Life*. Gainesville: University Press of Florida.

———. 2010. Identity and Collective Action in a Multiracial Community. *Historical Archaeology* 44 (1): 58–71.

———. 2011. *New Philadelphia: An Archaeology of Race in the Heartland*. Berkeley and Los Angeles: University of California Press.

———. 2013. A Historical Archaeology of Labor and Social Justice. *American Anthropologist* 115 (2): 317–320.

Shackel, Paul A., and David L. Larsen. 2000. Labor, Racism, and the Built Environment in Early Industrial Harpers Ferry. In *Lines that Divide: Historical Archaeologies of Race, Class, and Gender*, ed. James Delle, Robert Paynter, and Stephen Mrozowski, 22–39. Knoxville: University of Tennessee Press.

Shackel, Paul A., and Michael Roller. 2012. The Gilded Age Wasn't So Gilded in the Anthracite Region of Pennsylvania. *International Journal of Historical Archaeology* 16 (4): 761–775.

Shackel, Paul A., Michael Roller, and Kristin Sullivan. 2011. Historical Amnesia and the Lattimer Massacre. *Society for Historical Anthropology Newsletter*. http://sfaanews.sfaa.net/2011/05/01/historical-amnesia-and-the-lattimer-massacre/ (accessed 18 December 2012).

Shields, Mark. 1998. 'Made in the USA' Is at Heart of the Second Battle of Saipan. *Seattle Post-Intelligencer*, May 18, 1998, A7.

Shirky, Clay. 2003 Power Laws, Weblogs, and Inequality. http://www.shirky.com/writings/powerlaw_weblog.html (accessed May 8, 2013).

Silberman, Neil. 2008. Chasing the unicorn?: The quest for "essence" in digital heritage. In *New Heritage: New Media and Cultural Heritage*, ed. Yehuda E. Kalay, Thomas Kvan, and Janice Affleck, 81–91. New York: Routledge.

Silverman, Helaine, and D. Fairchild Ruggles. 2007. Cultural Heritage and Human Rights. In *Cultural Heritage and Human Rights*, ed. H. Silverman and D. F. Ruggles, 3–22. New York: Springer.

Simeone, James. 2000. *Democracy and Slavery in Frontier Illinois: The Bottomland Republic*. DeKalb: Northern Illinois University.

Smedley, Audrey. 1998 "Race" and the Construction of Human Identity. *American Anthropologist* 100 (3): 690–702.

Smith, Laurajane, Paul A. Shackel, and Gary Campbell. 2011. Introduction: Class Still Matters. In *Heritage, Labour and the Working Classes*, ed. Laurajane Smith, Paul A. Shackel, and Gary Campbell, 1-16. New York: Routledge.

Snodderly, Dan (editor). 2011. Peace Terms: Glossary of Terms for Conflict Management and Peacebuilding. Academy for International Conflict Management and Peacebuilding. Endowment of the United States Institute of Peace, Washington, DC. http://www.usip.org/peace_terms.pdf (accessed October 13, 2012).

Stahlgren, Lori C. 2012. Negotiating History, Slavery, and the Present: Archaeology at Farmington Plantation. In *Archaeologists as Activists: Can Archaeologists Change the World?*, ed. M. Jay Stottman, 95–109. Tuscaloosa: University of Alabama Press.

Starobin, Robert S. 1970. *Industrial Slavery in the Old South*. New York: Oxford University Press.

Su, Julie. 1997. El Monte Thai Garment Workers: Slave Sweatshops. In *No Sweat: Fashion Free Trade, and the Rights of Garment Workers*, ed. Andrew Ross, 143–149. New York: Verso.

Sullivan, Meg, and Edward North-Hager. 2008. Plan Brokered by Archaeologists Would Remove Roadblock to Mideast Peace. University of California, Los Angeles, press release. http://newsroom.ucla.edu/portal/ucla/plan-brokered-by-ucla-usc-archaeologists-47749.aspx (accessed August 22, 2008).

Sunstein, Cass R. 2004. *The Second Bill of Rights: Franklin Delano Roosevelt's Unfinished Revolution and Why We Need It More Than Ever*. New York: Basic Books.

Swidler, Nina, Kurt Dongoske, Roger Anyon, and Alan Downer, eds. 1997. *Native Americans and Archaeologists: Stepping Stones to Common Ground*. Walnut Creek, CA: AltaMira Press.

Tabane, Rapule. 2012. Lonmin Violence: It's D-Day for the Unions. *Mail and Guardian* August 17. http://mg.co.za/article/2012-08-17-00-d-day-for-the-unions (accessed December 4, 2012).

Tanner, Randy, Wayne Freimund, Brace Hayden, and Bill Dolan. 2007. The Waterton-Glacier International Peace Park: Conservation and Border Security. In Ali 2007, 183–199.

Thacker, Paul T. 2009. Archaeological Research within Community Service Learning Projects: Engagement, Social Action, and Learning from Happy Hill. In Nassaney and Levine 2009, 153–167.

Thomas, David H. 2000. *Skull wars: Kennewick Man, Archaeology, and the Battle for Native American Identity*. New York: Basic Books.

Tolbert, Caroline J., Ramona S. McNeal, and Daniel A. Smith. 2003. Enhancing Civic Engagement: The Effect of Direct Democracy on Political Participation and Knowledge. *State Politics and Policy Quarterly* 3 (1): 23–41.

Trouillot, Michel-Rolph. 1995. *Silencing the Past: Power and the Production of History*. Boston: Beacon Press.

Tutu, Desmond. 1999. *No Future without Forgiveness*. London: Rider.

Uddin, Sohel. 2013. Bangladesh Factory Collapse: Why Women Endure Danger to Make Clothes for the West. World News, NBC News.com. http://worldnews.nbcnews.com/_news/2013/05/26/18447688-bangladesh-factory-collapse-why-women-endure-danger-to-make-clothes-for-the-west?lite (accessed September 16, 2013).

United Nations Development Programme. 2012 *The Power of Local Action: Lessons from 10 Years of the Equator Prize*. New York: United Nations Development Programme.

United Nations Treaty Collection. 2013. Chapter IV. Human Rights. 3. International Covenant on Economic, Social and Cultural Rights. http://treaties.un.org/Pages/ViewDetails.aspx?src=TREATY&mtdsg_no=IV-3&chapter=4&lang=en. 4. International Covenant on Civil and Political Rights. http://treaties.un.org/Pages/ViewDetails.aspx?src=TREATY&mtdsg_no=IV-4&chapter=4&lang=en.

Vallejera, Jayvee L. 2007. NMI minimum Wage Hike OK'd. *Saipan Tribune.com*. May 27, 2007. http://www.saipantribune.com/newsstory.aspx?cat=1&newsID=68875 (accessed September 16, 2013).

Visweswaran, Kamala. 1998. Race and the Culture of Anthropology. *American Anthropologist* 100 (1): 70-83

Vogt, Jay D. 2007. The Kykuit II Summit: The Sustainability of Historic Sites. *History News* 62: 7–15.

Watkins, Joe. 2000. *Indigenous Archaeology: American Indian Values and Scientific Practice*. Walnut Creek, CA: AltaMira Press.

Weik, Terrance. 2012. *The Archaeology of Antislavery Resistance*. Gainesville: University Press of Florida.

White Deer, Gary. 2000. From Specimens to SAA Speakers: Evolution by Federal Mandate. In *Working Together: Native Americans and Archaeologists*, ed. Kurt E. Dongoske, Mark S. Aldenderfer, and Karen Doehner, 9–14. Washington, DC: Society for American Archaeology.

Williams, David. 2005. *A People's History of the Civil War: Struggles for the Meaning of Freedom*. New York: New Press.

Wilshire, Bruce. 1990. *The Moral Collapse of the University*. Albany: State University of New York Press.

Wysocki, Bernard, Jr. 1978. Review of *The Guns of Lattimer*, by Michael Novak. *Wall Street Journal*, December 13, 1978, 192.

Yankelovich, Daniel. 1991. *Coming to Public Judgment: Making Democracy Work in a Complex World*. Syracuse, NY: Syracuse University Press.

———. 1999. *The Magic of Dialogue: Transforming Conflict into Cooperation*. New York: Simon and Schuster.

———. 2010. How to Achieve Sounder Public Judgment. In *Toward Wiser Public Judgment*, ed. Will Friedman and Daniel Yankelovich, 11–32. Nashville, TN: Vanderbilt University Press.

Yankelovich, Daniel, and Will Friedman. 2010. How Americans Make Up Their Minds: The Dynamics of the Public's Learning Curve and Its Meaning for American Public Life. In *Toward Wiser Public Judgment*, ed. Will Friedman, and Daniel Yankelovich, 1–8. Nashville, TN: Vanderbilt University Press.

Zalasiewicz, Jan, Mark Williams, Alan Haywood, and Michael Ellis. 2011. The Anthropocene: A New Epoch of Geological Time? *Philosophical Transactions of the Royal Society A* 369: 835–841.

Index

About the Authors

Barbara J. Little is an Adjunct Professor of Anthropology and an Affiliate of the Center for Heritage Resource Studies at the University of Maryland, College Park. For twenty years she was an archaeologist with the U.S. National Park Service, where she is now the program manager for the cultural resources office of outreach. Dr. Little is particularly interested in the ways in which heritage is valued, recognized, and interpreted. She works in public archaeology on issues of public outreach and involvement, on the evaluation and official designations of archaeological places, and on the public relevance of archaeology. Her book, *Historical Archaeology: Why the Past Matters* (2007), was named an "Outstanding Academic Title" by *Choice* in 2008. In 2009, she delivered a lecture entitled "Reintegrating Archaeology in the Service of Sustainable Culture" as the Patty Jo Watson Distinguished Lecture in Archaeology at the American Anthropological Association meeting. She is the only federal archaeologist to be awarded this honor since this annual lecture was established in 1989.

Paul A. Shackel is Professor of Anthropology at the University of Maryland. His archaeology projects have focused on the role of archaeology in civic engagement activities. He co-edited a book on this topic titled *Archeology as a Tool of Civic Engagement* (AltaMira, 2007), with Barbara Little. He collaborated with other institutions to train undergraduates in archaeology to explore issues of race, class, and ethnicity on the Illinois western frontier at a biracial town known as New Philadelphia. Much of this work can be found in his book *New Philadelphia: An Archaeology of Race in the Heartland* (2011). He is currently engaged in developing a project that focuses on labor and immigration in northeastern Pennsylvania. The foundation for the project can be found in *The Archaeology of American Labor and Working Class Life* (2009b). His recent article with Michael Roller in the *International Journal of Historical Archaeology* entitled "The Gilded Age Wasn't So Gilded in the Anthracite Region of Pennsylvania" provides an overview of the project.